The Alps

Prepared by the Special Publications Division
National Geographic Society, Washington, D. C.

THE ALPS

Published by

THE NATIONAL GEOGRAPHIC SOCIETY
MELVIN M. PAYNE, *President*
MELVILLE BELL GROSVENOR, *Editor-in-Chief*
GILBERT M. GROSVENOR, *Editor*
ROBERT P. JORDAN, *Consulting Editor*

Contributing Authors and Photographers

JAMES P. BLAIR, WALTER MEAYERS EDWARDS,
  TOR EIGELAND, WILLIAM GRAVES,
  WILLIAM R. GRAY, MARY ANN HARRELL,
  ROBERT PAUL JORDAN, ARTHUR P. MILLER, JR.,
  GEORGE F. MOBLEY, CYNTHIA RUSS RAMSAY

Prepared by

THE SPECIAL PUBLICATIONS DIVISION
ROBERT L. BREEDEN, *Editor*
DONALD J. CRUMP, *Associate Editor*
PHILIP B. SILCOTT, *Senior Assistant Editor*
MARY ANN HARRELL, *Managing Editor*
LINDA M. BRIDGE, TUCKER L. ETHERINGTON,
  JANE MCCAULEY, *Research*

Illustrations

WILLIAM L. ALLEN, *Picture Editor*
  WILLIAM L. ALLEN, JAN N. CLARKSON,
  RONALD M. FISHER, WILLIAM R. GRAY,
  URSULA PERRIN, CYNTHIA RUSS RAMSAY,
  MICHAEL W. ROBBINS, *Picture Legends*

Layout and Design

JOSEPH A. TANEY, *Staff Art Director*
JOSEPHINE B. BOLT, *Art Director*
URSULA PERRIN, *Design Assistant*
JOHN D. GARST, JR., MONICA W. LEBEAU,
  MILDA RISSO-COLOMBO, *Map Research and
  Production*
TIBOR TOTH, *Map Art*
ROSALIE SEIDLER, *Coats of Arms for Chapter
  Titles*

Production and Printing

ROBERT W. MESSER, *Production Manager*
MARGARET MURIN SKEKEL, RAJA D. MURSHED,
  Production Assistants
JAMES R. WHITNEY, JOHN R. METCALFE, *Engraving
  and Printing*
MARTA ISABEL COONS, TONI EUGENE, SUZANNE J.
  JACOBSON, ELIZABETH VAN BEUREN JOY,
  PENELOPE A. LOEFFLER, JOAN PERRY, *Staff
  Assistants*
MARTHA HIGHTOWER, BARBARA KLEIN, *Index*

Library of Congress CIP Data page 207

*Overleaf: Ridgeline of the Mont Blanc massif juts
into an evening sky. Page 1: A dandelion pokes
through spring snow. Bookbinding: Emblem of the
Alps, edelweiss spreads lancelike leaves.*

NATIONAL GEOGRAPHIC PHOTOGRAPHER GEORGE F. MOBLEY
(OVERLEAF AND PAGE 1)

Masks and ornate headdresses disguise merrymakers

Foreword

THE WORD "AVALANCHE" has always con-
veyed a sense of terror. Yet, on one winter
trip to the Austrian Alps, the cry of *avalanche!*
brought cheerful results.

I was enjoying a ski holiday in the Alberg
region near Lech, when a fellow guest rushed
in with the news.

"We're marooned!" he exclaimed. "An avalanche has wiped out the road."

Those of us with business appointments
and planes to catch blanched—then relaxed.
The outside world might have thought us im-
prisoned for four days, but we knew better.
For now we came to know these Alpine
people as friends. Thanks to their neighbor-
liness, we enjoyed a magnificent feeling of

NATIONAL GEOGRAPHIC PHOTOGRAPHER GEORGE F. MOBLEY

at the Silvester-Klausen festival in Herisau, Switzerland—one of many traditional Alpine fetes.

mobility and self-reliance as we skied cross-country among the isolated villages. We understood, as never before, how freedom and independence grew naturally in the Alps.

For millenniums strong men have met the geographic challenge of these "savagely broken rocks"—so Livy describes them in his history of Hannibal's journey: "... it was worst for the pack-animals—loads and all, they went tumbling over the edge almost like falling masonry." Yet the great Carthaginian brought his army, with 37 battle elephants, to the summit and beyond.

"My men," Hannibal exhorted, "... you are walking over the very walls of Rome."

So they did. And no wonder that these natural walls inspired man's first scientific study of mountains.

I have traveled and worked in the mountain regions of all seven Alpine lands. The seasons can change in a matter of hours on an April drive from the last snows of Austria,

through the Brenner Pass, into an Italian springtime. Even the people seem to change with the temperature. But if tempers and customs vary from one valley to the next, the mountains inspire a special, transcending spirit. Language aside, an Alpine Frenchman may have more in common with a Slovenian mountain man than with a lowlander of his own country.

Before technology works its havoc, I have two Alpine ambitions. First, some spring I want to follow a herdsman as he takes his cattle from the valley up to mountain pastures. My other hope is to spend part of a winter with a traditional farm family. Meantime, I shall enjoy the same experiences in the pages of this book. Here eight authors look beyond the postcard scenery to show us the everyday adventure of families who live and work in these mountains year round. Here are the *human* Alps.

GILBERT M. GROSVENOR

5

Knifing through a jagged realm of white, a skier trails a powdery plume on Switzerland's Corvatsch above

Contents

St. Moritz, a resort—like many in the Alps—that throngs with skiers and climbers, tourists and jet-setters.

1

"COME ON, you *have* to climb at least one," a friend insisted at Zermatt. I was delighted with the village and the view—"the very sanctuary of the 'Spirit of the Alps,'" says a 1903 guidebook on Switzerland. And I was entirely content with hikers' paths that don't force you to hang on with your hands. My friend had just completed a practice climb on one of the easier peaks before he took on the 14,690-foot-high Matterhorn. He had not quite convinced me when the conversation drifted to the problem of replacing his sunglasses: "They fell off."

"Why didn't you pick them up?"

"They fell 900 feet." That was convincing. You don't necessarily have to climb the Alps to enjoy them.

"Playground of Europe," climber and scholar Leslie Stephen called the Alps a century ago. Now the phrase would be "Playground of the World."

From the Maritime Alps with their views of the Mediterranean to the Vienna Woods, from Bavaria to Lake Bled, the mountains sustain an empire of entertainment. Bikini-wearing skiers in Italy, hitchhiking students, architecture buffs, music lovers assembling at Salzburg, climbers from Mexico or Japan, Middle Westerners game enough to stretch their throats on a yodel—all of them can find diversions in the diversity of the Alps.

Long before I ever saw the clear dazzle of Alpine snowfields, I met the high pastures and white peaks as part of Heidi's world. Like so many other children, I knew that "Alps" meant the life of the herdsmen.

In fact I saw my first snow mountains as a backdrop for the formal gardens by Lake Como; goat-herding seemed wildly remote from the neatly trimmed hedges, the stone figures in classic drapery and the living figures in casual drip dry with garlands of cameras. As an introduction to the human variety of the Alps, it was perfect.

"In the Rockies," says a colleague thoughtfully, "you're aware of a land that goes on for hundreds of miles; in the Alps you're aware of a life that has gone on for hundreds of years—how a particular village or city has developed its own particular ways over the centuries."

Dimensions alone *(Continued on page 25)*

Alpine Grandeur at Europe's Heart

By MARY ANN HARRELL

At Appenzell, Switzerland, not far from Heidi country, an elder contentedly leans from a sliding window of his 200-year-old home.

NATIONAL GEOGRAPHIC PHOTOGRAPHER GEORGE F. MOBLEY

Cross-country skiers—some 4,000 strong—begin the 26-mile Engadine Skimarathon, held in March. Anyone

who registers may enter. Surname determines starting position; best overall time to the finish line means victory.

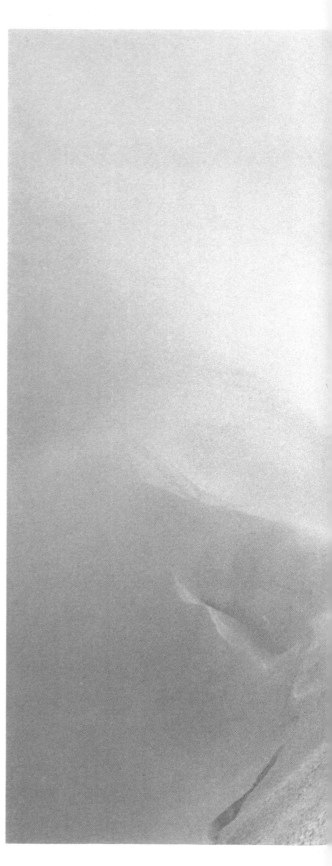

Eyeing an abyss, a short-haired St. Bernard named Seine demonstrates the alertness that made her life-saving ancestors famous. Here in the Great St. Bernard Pass, between Switzerland and Italy, Benedictine monks like Father Bennard have maintained a hospice for nearly 1,000 years. Dogs — with their keen ears and noses — once helped find lost travelers; rescue services today rely largely on helicopters. At right, Swiss soldiers on winter training exercises trudge along the highest ridge of Piz Palu in the Bernina Alps.

N.G.S. PHOTOGRAPHER JAMES P. BLAIR (ABOVE) AND ROBI O. HUGENTOBLER

"Never fly higher than you'd like to fall," experienced members of the kite-skiing fraternity caution beginners. Here an airborne skier glides above jagged peaks of the French Alps. An expert, strapped to a trapeze beneath the kite and maneuvering with guy wires attached to the wings, can stay aloft 15 or 20 minutes. A tobogganist (left) launches himself on the famed Cresta Run at St. Moritz, Switzerland. On bare-boned sleds called "skeletons," riders hurtle down the winding chute at 80 miles an hour or more.

"A dome standing brilliant in the firmament," 19th-century Slovene writer Julius Kugy said of Mont Blanc,

at 15,771 feet the highest mountain in the chain. Here climbers follow a sinuous trail on a sun-brushed flank.

Patchwork of fields and meadows encircles Wiesing, a quiet village in the Tyrolean Alps of Austria. The River Inn flows down its namesake valley toward a junction with the Danube. A villager rakes a freshly mown May harvest, then drapes the hay in thumb-shaped piles on drying racks. Near St. Johann, another Tyrolean village, a young girl schools a jumper on a longeing rein.

Craggy fastness high in the French Alps near Chamonix faces the warming sun. "Bare, wild and sublime," wrote Mary Shelley in her novel The Last Man.

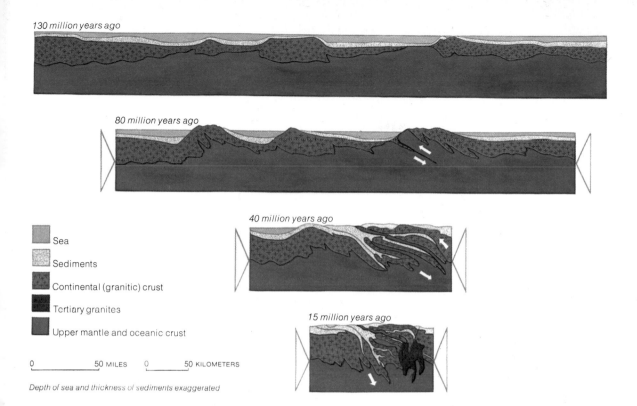

130 million years ago

80 million years ago

40 million years ago

15 million years ago

Sea

Sediments

Continental (granitic) crust

Tertiary granites

Upper mantle and oceanic crust

0 ____ 50 MILES   0 ____ 50 KILOMETERS

Depth of sea and thickness of sediments exaggerated

AS AGES PASS, STUPENDOUS FORCES COMPRESS THE REGION OF THE ALPS: A NORTH-SOUTH CROSS SECTION NARROWS FROM 400 MILES OR SO TO 75

The Alps owe their complicated geology to two related phenomena: the spreading of ocean floors and the ponderous sliding of continents, borne upon gigantic raftlike plates, about the earth. As recently as 130 million years ago a body of water called the Tethys Sea covered a region (top panel) between the African and Eurasian plates. On the floor of this sea a thick layer of sediment accumulated. Meanwhile, physical changes elsewhere—probably affecting the entire planet—were producing compression that would shrink the Tethys Sea enormously.

Although continental drift had been suspected in the 1920's, only in recent decades have geologists found convincing evidence that huge plates of crustal rock are indeed in motion. In the 1950's they began to chart a mountain chain 40,000 miles long on the floor of the major oceans, rimming the globe like stitching on a baseball. In this chain molten rock continually emerges from within the earth. As it does, the ocean floor spreads, carrying the continents along as on a conveyor belt.

By this process (second panel), the African plate on the right and the Eurasian plate are squeezed together. Islands emerge from the Tethys Sea. Where the plates meet (arrows), a process of subduction has begun: the Eurasian plate turns downward, overridden by the African. The third panel reveals the structure existing about 40 million years ago. Compression—at the rapid rate of about two inches per year—has created an interfingering of sediment and crust.

Finally, 15 million years ago, the Alpine region reaches more or less its present dimensions and complex state (fourth panel). The crust thickens; molten crustal granite rises by its own buoyancy; subduction goes on. About 5 million years ago—yesterday in geologic time—strong uplift raised miles-high mountains here; erosion has shaped them into the Alps we know today. The Wildhauser-Schafberg peak in Switzerland (opposite), folded and uplifted 5 million years ago, exhibits layers of limestone from sediment deposited 100 million years ago in the now-vanished Tethys Sea.

cannot account for the richness of the Alps. This whole range would fit easily into Virginia and West Virginia combined. Measured along the arc from Nice to Vienna, the length of the chain is some 650 miles. Its width is surprisingly narrow, averaging only 100 miles. Overall, the Alpine area occupies 80,000 square miles: modest, as mountain systems go. In contrast, the Rockies extend roughly 3,000 miles in length, with a maximum width of 350 miles or so. The young Himalayas run some 1,500 by 150 miles.

Nevertheless, the Alps may well be the most famous of major mountain ranges and are certainly the most thoroughly examined. Here, in the 19th century, the scientific study of mountains began. Thus the Alps became a standard—but this, warns geologist Rudolf Trümpy of Zurich, can be misleading, considering the complexity and great variety of mountain-building events.

Why mountains ever rose at all has perplexed and distressed men in the past. Although the Scriptures speak of the Lord's holy mountain, early Jewish and Christian scholars often blamed the origin of mountains on sin. Some cited the disobedience of Adam and Eve; others, Cain's murder of Abel; others, the general corruption that provoked the flood in Noah's time. Nothing less calamitous could have replaced good farmland with useless heaps of rock and ice.

But beauty? Anyone who visits the Alps must keep memories of scenes that brought absolute exultation. I recall such classic vistas as the Matterhorn beyond the glaciers from Gornergrat; but most vivid of all is a single white summit, sunlit above a valley in gathering dusk, unforgettable even though its name has faded with the name of the Swiss restaurant that served delectable fresh-caught trout for dinner that night.

Yet for generations men found the Alps—and other mountains—ugly. Latin poets called the Alps "frozen" or "savage" if they wrote of them at all. Compiling adjectives for mountains in the 1670's, an Englishman included a few like "lovely, star-brushing," but more in this vein: "insolent, surly, barren, pathless, melancholy, forsaken, crump-shouldered."

Probably the fatigue and risk of travel inspired some of this. A young Welshman

Mer de Glace—*Sea of Ice*—*flows beneath climbers on l'Aiguille du Marne. Ripples form as the glacier crosses broken ground.*

wrote in 1621: "I am now got over the Alps ...I had crossed and clambered up the Pyreneans to Spain before; they are not so high and hideous as the Alps...." In 1646 diarist John Evelyn, riding muleback in Switzerland's Simplon Pass, found it "very steepe, craggy, & dangerous ... onely inhabited with Beares, Wolves, & Wild Goates...."

Travel was still tiring, however, when 18th-century visitors seeing the Alps for the first time declared themselves "rapt" in the face of the sublime, and when 19th-century strangers marveled at the vast glories of the Alps and leafed through the pages of Byron or Shelley for words to express so great a thrill: "All that expands the spirit, yet appals / Gather around these summits." Or: "... all seems eternal now."

APPALLING PRESENCES had haunted the Alps far earlier. According to legend, the accursed body of Pontius Pilate wound up at Lausanne; in desperation the citizens dumped it into a little lake on Mount Pilatus. Pilate's ghost ceased to give trouble only after 1585, when Pastor Johann Müller of Lucerne led some valiant skeptics to hurl rocks into the water—and returned safely.

Dragons survived longer. The learned Professor Johann Jacob Scheuchzer of Zurich (1672-1733) weighed the sworn testimony of honest men who had seen them, and concluded that Alpine dragons vary greatly in appearance. He never had the good luck to see one for himself; monsters have apparently grown rarer as climbers have grown more numerous.

Just who could properly claim the title of first modern mountaineer is subject to dispute, but nobody questions the role of the Alps as birthplace of climbing for pleasure. In 1786 Dr. Michel-Gabriel Paccard and Jacques Balmat were first to reach the summit of Mont Blanc; thereafter increasing numbers of men—and women—risked the perils of strange peaks, unpredictable storms and rockfalls, altitude sickness, and panic.

By the mid-19th century a summer holiday in the Alps had become a recognized luxury —for the minority rich enough to afford it. Winter holidays grew fashionable after 1864, when Herr Johannes Badrutt, owner of the Kulm Hotel in St. Moritz, invited four Englishmen to visit him in December at his own expense. Perhaps to their own astonishment, they enjoyed themselves. Hotel, village, and the entire Alpine region were entering a

GASTON REBUFFAT, RAPHO GUILLUMETTE

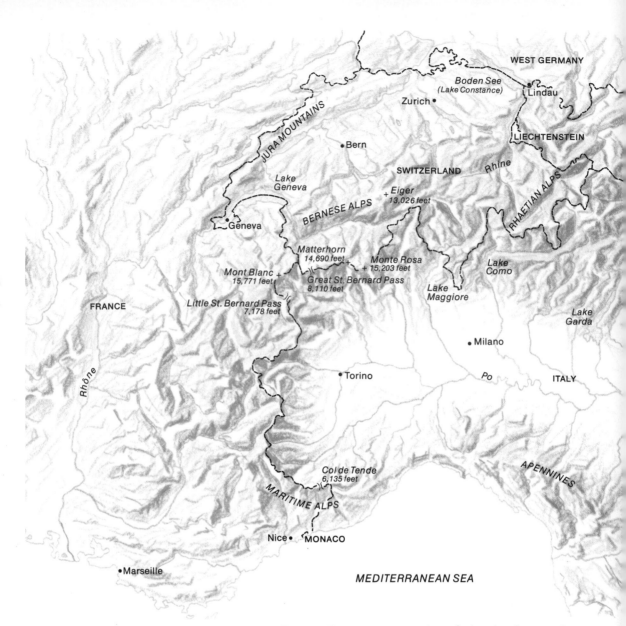

WEST GERMANY

Boden See
(Lake Constance)

Lindau

Zurich

JURA MOUNTAINS

Bern

LIECHTENSTEIN

SWITZERLAND

Rhine

Lake
Geneva

RHAETIAN ALPS

Eiger
13,026 feet

BERNESE ALPS

Geneva

Matterhorn
14,690 feet

Monte Rosa
+ 15,203 feet

Lake
Como

Mont Blanc +
15,771 feet

Great St. Bernard Pass
8,110 feet

Lake
Maggiore

Lake
Garda

Little St. Bernard Pass
7,178 feet

FRANCE

Milano

Torino

Po

ITALY

Rhône

Col de Tende
6,135 feet

APENNINES

MARITIME ALPS

Nice   MONACO

Marseille

MEDITERRANEAN SEA

Seven European countries—Switzerland, France, Liechtenstein, Germany, Italy, Yugoslavia, and Austria—share the Alps, a mountain chain small by Himalayan or Andean standards but enormous in its wealth of romance, grandeur, and human history.

distinctively new era: a century of sport.

Even the name Alps carries a hint that for generations life in this region was severely practical. Apparently the Latin *Alpes* owes something to a Celtic word *Alb*, which may mean "white" or may mean "height"; but in local speech an alp was always a high pasture where cattle or sheep or goats could feed in summer.

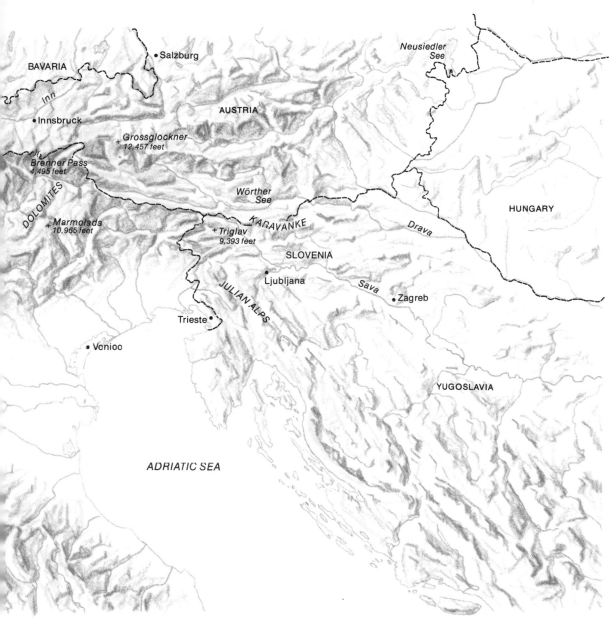

Taking the stock upland in late spring, bringing them down to lower pastures in autumn ... that cycle has outlived the Roman Empire, the brief empire of Napoleon, who shook the states in and around and beyond the Alps, the long empire of the Habsburgs. Today the old life of the pastures supplies an attraction for something utterly new: the economy of tourism.

Thousands upon thousands of men and women, traveling just for pleasure—nothing really of this magnitude has happened before, in the Alps or elsewhere. And if prosperity brings visitors, visitors bring good fortune; the paying guest leaves an Alpine farm family happily planning to buy something new.

I would hate to try to choose a single favorite spot among the Alps, but selecting a tribute is easier. An uncomplicated one, it comes from a hunchback villager named Luk Meynet. To support the widow and children of his dead brother, he was willing to go as a porter with the English climber Edward Whymper in three of his attempts to climb the Matterhorn, "unconquerable" until Whymper's final success in 1865. Whymper told how he and Luk Meynet reached the Col du Lion, at the foot of the mountain's southwest ridge, and saw the great peak close and unclouded for the first time: "The poor little deformed peasant gazed upon it silently and reverently ... and then unconsciously fell on one knee and clasped his hands, exclaiming in ecstasy, 'Oh, beautiful mountains!'" □

THE BELL CLANGED three times, signaling misfortune. I glanced unhappily down the treacherous Cresta Run at St. Moritz, a first-time tobogganer waiting to challenge the Swiss Alps. Buehler, an experienced rider, had just soared out over an icy vertical curve, tumbling through the air like a rag doll. "I say, Buehler," demanded the starter's crisp voice on the loudspeaker. "Wave an arm if you're all right. Good man. Thank you." No broken bones, then. It does happen.

"Jordan." Clipped summons. "Are you there?" I fastened my crash helmet, adjusted my goggles, tightened protective leather pads covering knees and elbows, checked metal guards shielding my hands. Into the frozen run I stepped, belly-flopped on my sled—a small, bare vehicle called a "skeleton," without brakes or steering—and pushed off. Down that serpentine chute the skeleton carried me, committed, ever faster, chin six inches off the ground. Body English, one desperate, instinctive lurch after another, must negotiate those sheer banked turns.

Great Cresta runners have approached 90 miles an hour along the three-quarter-mile course. Beginners like myself, who must start at "the Junction" about 450 yards below the top, can safely reach speeds of 30 or so. But who's trying to be safe? I don't know my peak velocity; only that in a mind-blanking blur I skimmed across the finish line, most grateful to reach it—drained, trembling, then exhilarated, even euphoric. Later I realized that the harrowing run also provided an introduction to the real magic of Switzerland. Emboldened, I rode the Cresta once again, chopped nearly ten seconds off my previous time, and knew the magic once more.

Happily, it is a gift freely bestowed, which explains why this small, landlocked country in the heart of Europe has lured the world's pleasure seekers for so long. Quite simply, the Swiss Alps transport us out of our humdrum selves.

In some ways, as I have learned well, this has to do with gravity, the physical trammels of earth, which skiers throw off as they swoop down snow-gleaming mountain flanks, and which alpinists surmount to achieve their summits. But the gift is given also to hikers strolling deep (Continued on page 49)

Dominated by the 14,690-foot Matterhorn, the village of Zermatt offers strenuous mountain climbing—or leisured mountain viewing.

2

Switzerland: The Gifts of Mountain Freedom

By ROBERT PAUL JORDAN
Photographs by JAMES P. BLAIR

Battery-powered wipers sweep the lenses of a skier on Corvatsch, a peak above St. Moritz. Most famous of Swiss ski resorts, St. Moritz has attracted devotees since the mid-1800's with "good air, good snow, good sport." At right, guests gather après-ski in the Disco Club. Cornetists participate in ceremonies to welcome medalists returning from the 1972 Winter Olympics in Japan.

NATIONAL GEOGRAPHIC PHOTOGRAPHER JAMES P. BLAIR (BELOW AND RIGHT)

NATIONAL GEOGRAPHIC PHOTOGRAPHER GEORGE F. MOBLEY (BELOW)

32

Content as a bystander, Mrs. Gunter Sachs watches her industrialist husband compete in the Cresta Club's toboggan race; nearby the Empress of Iran races through slalom gates of the exclusive Corviglia Ski Club. At lower left, a Swiss team hurtles down the chute during the European Bobsled Championship. A member of the Fullplast Acrobatic Ski Team (below) back-somersaults gracefully off a ramp less than six feet high.

ADAM WOOLFITT

33

Ribbons of copper clouds streak the dawn sky over Switzerland's Alps. "The palaces of Nature," Byron called these awesome peaks.

With fascinated children for an audience, a hot-air balloon begins a dangerous flight across the Alps from Zermatt to Cervinia, Italy, in August 1972. Before this first successful hot-air crossing, the two pilots consulted an Alpine meteorologist and devoted time and money to other safety precautions. During a more orthodox crossing a sunburst seems to shatter a helicopter's windscreen.

Sunshot forest — a cathedral of calm — clothes an Alpine slope in repose. Statuesque stag (below), a fallow deer, stands in a shaft of sunlight in the Riegelsee Wildlife Park in the Canton of Bern. A magistrate of remarkable foresight — Joachim Baldi — created Switzerland's first wildlife refuge in 1548, the still-inviolate Karpf Game Reserve in the Canton of Glarus. The 45,500-acre Swiss National Park on the Italian border, established in 1914, protects the rare chamois, long hunted for sport and for the versatile "shammy" made from its soft, pliable skin.

FRANZ VILLIGER, GSTAAD (RIGHT)

Violin virtuoso Yehudi Menuhin rehearses before 15th-century frescoes in the choir of the
Saanen church, dating from 1444. Each year
in late summer artists gather in Saanen — near
the popular resort town of Gstaad — for the
three-week-long Menuhin Festival. The valleys around Saanen once witnessed clan-
destine Masses, as stubborn Catholics re-
sisted the Reformation. Not far away, strollers
ramble the grassy summit of the Wispillen.

Alpine Festival at Aeschiried offers a break in the toil and tedium of harvesting and herding. The midsummer Festival lets visitors glimpse Swiss traditions, but serves primarily as an excuse for local people to gather in celebration. Alpenhorns 12 feet long resound; neighbors consume beer and sausages, join in yodeling and group singing, and watch flag tossing and Schwingen — Swiss wrestling. Spectators rim a sawdust circle where their sons and grandsons battle.

Darkness of a mid-July storm edges toward Aeschi. Peaks of the Bernese Oberland — Sigriswiler Rothorn (left)

and Niederhorn—rise beyond. New-mown meadows await the return of cattle now in high summer pastures.

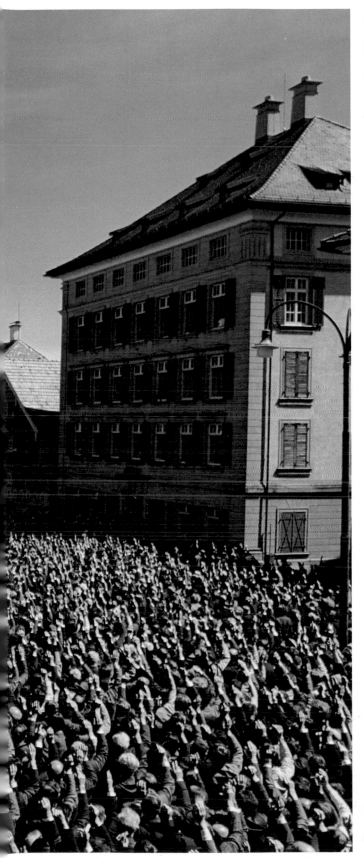

Continuing a 600-year-old tradition of direct democracy, men of Appenzell at the annual Landsgemeinde (constitutional assembly) in Trogen vote on public issues. Only men, from age 20 on, take part. To begin, each raises his right hand and vows allegiance to the Constitution. After electing officials, the men decide current legislative proposals. The first Landsgemeinde met in Glarus in 1387. To symbolize their right to vote, men still carry swords (above) or daggers, while a junior honor-guard member too young to vote gazes quizzically at the proceedings.

green valleys and high flower-tossed meadows, and to those who only gaze in wonder at serrated massifs marching endlessly away into the sky. It is the gift of freedom.

The Alps must also have powerful impact on the 5.3 million Swiss citizens. Splitting Europe all the way from France to Yugoslavia, these mountains unify Switzerland—and yet, paradoxically, few peoples are more diverse. "We *are* different," said Hans Muller, a diplomat serving as cultural attaché. "Our economic and social opinions are not so different as you might expect; but in our daily life and temperament we do vary greatly from one valley, village, city, and canton [state] to the next. We have no single national personality."

I will not dispute Mr. Muller. Traveling the country over, I heard many people mix languages in mid-sentence. Far more, however, had difficulty understanding one another. Consider: about 68 percent speak Swiss-German dialects, some quite dissimilar; about 19 percent converse in French; about 11 percent talk in Italian; and a comparative handful use Rhaeto-Romansh, a language rooted in Latin antiquity. Superimpose on this cacophony the voices of a million foreign workers (thriving, highly industrialized Switzerland lists about 100 jobless) and you may think you have landed in Babel.

Hard-working, conservative, thrifty, tolerant, refreshingly honest—these attributes have helped the Swiss attain the world's fourth highest per capita income, after the United States, Canada, and Sweden.

Above all else, the Swiss treasure their hard-won right to live in peace. For nearly twenty centuries their forebears warred among themselves and were warred over by invaders from Julius Caesar to Napoleon. Then, in 1815, the Treaties of Vienna and Paris declared permanent Swiss neutrality to be in the interest of all Europe.

To ensure that neutrality, every able-bodied man trains as a citizen-soldier, keeps his own weapon at home, and knows his mobilization assignment. Within 48 hours, 620,000 men can be called up. Every strategic bridge and tunnel can be blown to bits on order. "You see," Hans Muller summed up succinctly, "our neutrality is our freedom."

Pledging unity against oppression, actors in the William Tell play at Interlaken re-create the Swiss Confederation's founding in 1291.

Switzerland then is the name of nearly 16,000 blessed square miles of peaks and valleys, plateaus and forests; Pennsylvania spreads about three times larger. At its longest, this jumbled land extends 226 miles; at its widest, 127. One day I would ride an electric train almost to the top of the central Bernese Oberland for one of Europe's grandest views, a humbling panorama of snowy ramparts sweeping south into Italy, north across the low Jura Mountains into the Black Forest. That spectacle would encompass a country half given over to farms and pastures, a fourth to trees, and the rest to cities and industry, to lakes, glaciers, and rocks.

But what lakes: Geneva of the gentle waters and the storied castle of Chillon in moon-glowing mist; Lugano, dancing in sunshine, fringed with palms and mimosa. And glaciers: the Grosse Aletsch, 17-mile river of ice, longest in all the Alps; many other frozen streams, some flecked in summer with bikini-clad skiers. And the rocks....

IN THE FIRST PART of my first trip to Switzerland, at dawn in the old village of Zermatt, I looked nearly two miles overhead to see the towering, Sphinx-like Matterhorn take the sun's fire, while a blizzard wreathed its granite crown in gossamer white. The words of an early beholder came to mind: "It has the appearance of a frowning Deity who would forbid the approach of mortal feet."

Later that winter day my ski instructor, a solid, even-dispositioned man of 60 named Oskar Perren, set me straight. He caught me staring at the jagged peak and read my mind. "*Ja,* you can climb it," he assured me. "Come back next summer. I will guide you to the top." It would not be very difficult provided I were in good condition, he said.

Oskar Perren lighted a cigar and squinted at me with pale blue eyes. "I first climbed the Matterhorn when I was 18. I have been 235 times to the summit."

Subsequently, toiling in his ski class, I wished more than once that I was scaling that steep, frowning rock face instead. My fellow learners offered some small consolation; they too fell, and fell, and fell. The patient Perren ignored the perversity of our skis.

"Loook hee-er. Hee-er. Do eet like theese," he coaxed, demonstrating a graceful turn. "So-o-o e-e-easy," he intoned, coasting to a toed-in "snowplow" halt. Gradually we began to win dabs of praise: "Dot ees gut." And finally: "Ja, tomorrow we go up and ski."

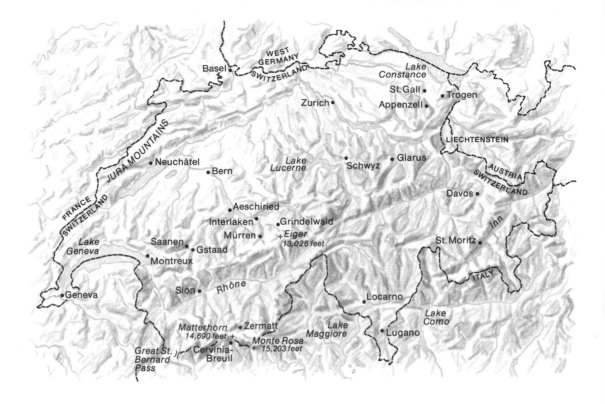

Map labels:
WEST GERMANY · SWITZERLAND · Basel · Lake Constance · St. Gall · Trogen · Zurich · Appenzell · LIECHTENSTEIN · JURA MOUNTAINS · Neuchâtel · Lake Lucerne · Schwyz · Glarus · AUSTRIA · SWITZERLAND · Bern · Davos · Inn · FRANCE · SWITZERLAND · Aeschiried · Interlaken · Grindelwald · Mürren · +Eiger 13,026 feet · St. Moritz · Saanen · Gstaad · Lake Geneva · Montreux · Sion · Rhône · Locarno · Lake Como · ITALY · Geneva · Lake Maggiore · Lugano · Matterhorn 14,690 feet + · Zermatt · Monte Rosa + 15,203 feet · Great St. Bernard Pass · Cervinia-Breuil

Mecca of mountaineers, playground of sportsmen, a rugged Alpine backbone unifies diverse Switzerland. A realm of grumbling glaciers and their offspring lakes, the mountains cover nearly one-fourth of the country.

Skiers converge on Zermatt from near and far, attracted by the fame of 40-odd *pistes*, or ski runs, that twist down the surrounding mountains. "Who are your visitors?" I asked Constant Cachin, Zermatt's genial tourism director. He rattled off his statistics: "30 percent are Swiss; Germans make up 21 percent; Americans, 19 percent; English, 10 percent; French, 9 percent; Japanese, 2.4 percent; and 'miscellaneous' accounts for the rest. The average tourist spends at least 100 Swiss francs a day [about $25]."

Like me, many visitors are agreeably surprised by the town's most unusual traffic statistic: no automobiles. Winter guests hop from the valley-climbing cog train into horse-drawn sleighs; snug in lap robes they glide to their hotels and *pensions*.

Should it chance to be night, the town seems something out of a fairy tale. Falling snow thickens on rooftops and diffuses the soft glow from shop windows, church bells toll the hour, chalets and huts dispense twinkles of light, bits and pieces of drifting talk bespeak many homelands—*merci*... *jawohl*... *bene*... good night.

Tomorrows, I discovered, all thanks to ski instructor Perren, are fine on the runs above Zermatt. And I think that most of the thousands of skiers who tried the slopes with me would say the same. Up we rode by railway, chairlift, cable car, draglift—each seeking out the pistes that suited his skill, or his courage. Then down we flew, some of us taking a header here and there, but that was part of the game. Weary, we rested at tiny mountain inns and quaffed *Bier* or soft drinks. At lunchtime we thronged large cafeterias and put away immense quantities of soup, salad, sausages, potatoes. Revived, we clamped skis back on and rode up to favored starting points. All day we coursed the heights, and forgot ourselves.

Still, I liked as much the *après-ski* hours. With NATIONAL GEOGRAPHIC photographer James P. Blair I walked Zermatt's narrow streets, past humming hotels and restaurants, *Stuben* (taverns), well-stocked boutiques and sports shops, and jewelry stores with tempting displays of some of the world's finest watches. In Switzerland, watchmaker nonpareil, time is money.

A holidaying crowd jostled about us, laughing, boisterous; this famed resort draws many fun-loving, unselfconscious young people. Other centers appeal to different clienteles. Some are known for winter sports; some for summer relaxation; some for both. "In the Swiss Alps," Jim Blair observed, "there is something for *everybody*."

One thing pleased Jim and me wherever we traveled: the food. In spotless small cafés and velvet-draped halls of *haute cuisine* alike, we enjoyed excellent fare and service. And flowers invariably graced the table. "When you write about Switzerland," Jim said, "don't forget the flowers."

With food and drink holding to a high standard (Swiss table wines, especially the light white Fendant and the mild red Dôle, win increasing appreciation), the trick in making the most of an Alpine vacation is to discover the resort that suits you best. If you are young and well-heeled, Gstaad's fast-moving, chalet-partying social scene may be the answer. In Davos or any of a host of enclaves where informality prevails, you can be chic or not for après-ski festivities, as you please. In the south, in Lugano or Locarno, you can bask in a mild Mediterranean clime

and spice it with Italian cooking. At Montreux and Interlaken, havens for the British since the 19th century, await vast, comfortable, well-run, nobly Victorian hotels, soul-satisfying vistas of lake and mountains, and an easy, orderly pace.

Above Interlaken, riding the cogwheel "Jungfrau Express," you pierce a far-flung world of eternal snow where giants stand in ranks: the Blümlisalp, Bietschhorn, Schreckhorn, others. These trail away as mere lordlings to the mighty three-headed majesty of rock and ice towering over you: the man-killing Eiger (Ogre), 13,026 feet; the tractable Mönch (Monk), 13,449 feet; the bulky Jungfrau (Virgin), 13,642 feet.

I HAVE ATTENDED these mountains, awed, both winter and summer. Beneath their summits on a brilliant February day I watched hordes of skiers streak downward, a happy cavalcade darting along 60 miles of marked runs. Perky little electric trains carried as many as 12,000 passengers an hour coming and going from Interlaken and Alpine resort villages like Mürren, Lauterbrunnen, Wengen, and Grindelwald.

Always my eyes returned to the grim, convexly curving north face of the Eiger, one of the Alps' most compelling sights. Only since 1935 have climbers assaulted this mile-high, sheer, ice-hung, malevolent wall; many have died in the attempt. "Mountain of death," I said to my guide, Walter Gertsch, when in June we stood before it. At 43, strongly built, deep-voiced, Walter had spent his adult life skiing, climbing, and guiding tourists in this region. He nodded darkly at the Eiger and spoke his mind:

"In summer he is active all day, that one. He lives. He is mad. It does not matter how good a climber you are. How can you tell if the lightning storm comes? Who can know when the avalanche falls, or the piece of glacier breaks off? What can you offer against the blizzard? There is no one who can say, 'I am going to climb the Eiger, and I am coming back.' You do not handle him. He handles you."

I lunched that day at 11,333-foot Jungfraujoch, Europe's highest railway station, and then walked out on the glacier that falls from the plateau between the Mönch and the Jungfrau. A summer snowstorm swirled about me, wind-driven, and I could see only a short distance. It was unwise to proceed far, and quite suddenly I grew uneasy in the silence. I hurried back into the warm station. How lonely it must be for the men and women who pit themselves against the Eiger.

Yet that is the story of the Swiss Alps— something for everybody. Walter Gertsch extols the attractions of the Bernese Oberland; other guides speak as highly of *their* dominions. Internationally, the king of Swiss playgrounds remains St. Moritz, though not all see it my way. Once, in another part of the country, I suggested to a young ski instructor that he might enjoy working in St. Moritz. Like most Swiss, he was candid: "I would not teach those people. They are snobs. They are very rich. They wear very expensive ski boots—but do not leave the bar."

In this exaggeration rests the usual modicum of truth. But most rich denizens of St. Moritz *do* ski the slopes of the Corviglia, Corvatsch, and Piz Nair; some fly to secluded runs by chartered airplane or helicopter. Certainly wealth counts in St. Moritz. It is even better to be titled. The roster of the formidably exclusive Corviglia Ski Club— membership limited to 160—lists some of the world's most famous titles and fortunes; its Committee includes the Duc de Sangro, Comte Theo Rossi de Montelera, the Duke of Marlborough, Arnold von Bohlen und Halbach, Prince Constantin de Liechtenstein.

I saw plainly, for all this, that thousands of us lesser lights also feel perfectly at ease on the slopes here. And the St. Moritz Tobogganing Club, proudly democratic, opens the Cresta Run for a small fee to everyone who seeks its camaraderie of shared fright. (Everyone, that is, except women, who are forbidden to ride the course. Make what you will of the sign in the club's locker room: "Where women cease from troubling and the wicked are at rest.")

In short, a stratified democracy pervades St. Moritz; it has room for all, offering a wide range of prices, accommodations, and activities. A small downtown grocery nicely reflects this catholicity. Across the front it proclaims: "Kaffee Tea Caviar."

For more than half a century, Prince Constantin de Liechtenstein has returned each year to St. Moritz. "This is my second home," he told me. "In winter, it has the best weather, on average, of all Europe. Good air, good snow, good sport."

At his invitation, I called on the Prince at his modest third-floor flat above a busy thoroughfare. A widower, tall and tanned, informal in slacks and sweater, he answered the door and greeted me with a handshake and a smile. We looked out on the Upper Engadine Valley where Alpine peaks dominate an ice-covered lake, and I asked what particular attraction St. Moritz held for him.

"This is the nicest place of anywhere to come in winter," Prince Constantin said. "In most resorts, skiing is the one big thing. Here you can do all sorts of sports—there is even horse racing on the frozen lake. This fantastic, big, broad, open valley you will not find in the rest of Europe."

He paused, reflecting. "In winter St. Moritz is still the best. But it is getting overbuilt, overpopulated. Some of the buildings were always ugly, but they get uglier."

TO ME, the old buildings were part of its charm. Not far up the street stood the world-famous, turreted Palace Hotel, which opened in 1896. "I have a warm feeling for the Palace," said Prince Constantin. "It keeps up to date, and yet remains the same."

Today, many of the anointed purchase their own villas in St. Moritz. (An unimproved half-acre lot, choicely located, can cost a million Swiss francs—roughly $250,000.) The Aga Khan and the Shah of Iran and their retinues maintained private residences during my stay. Year in and out, the Palace continues as the focal point, the gathering place for jet setters, the titled, captains of commerce and industry, government figures, movie stars, playboys and playgirls, and those who are intrigued by this passing parade.

I lodged at the Palace, intrigued, and enjoyed its hospitality—most of all the late afternoons and early evenings spent in its elegant, crowded, great hall. All about me the beautiful people made preprandial devotions, taking tea and apéritifs, chatting against the gentle intrusion of a tinkling piano, table-hopping in ski pants, Italian silk blouses, cashmere sweaters, mink coats. Presently I would put après-ski ambiance behind to plunge into the Palace's new two-million-dollar pool; once I donned black tie for late dinner, and then attended a glittering gala. Other times I watched perfervid bridge players study their cards: they had good reason. As an onlooker beside me said, "The smallest stakes are ten cents a point."

When the time came to leave St. Moritz, I paid my respects to Andrea Badrutt, the slim, energetic, engaging man who with his brother Hansjürg directs the Palace as did their father and his father before them. "How do you keep in the forefront?" I asked. "Four hundred beds, four hundred employees, some of the most demanding guests on earth...."

"We give them what they want, and we do not change," he replied briskly, flipping his glasses high on his forehead. "We modernize in the best way possible, but we keep the elegance, the glamor. The people who come here are leaders in fashion, art, finance—in everything that makes life more than a dreary fight from day to day. For them life must be gay, amusing. We have to give them something they can find nowhere else."

It is Andrea Badrutt, greeting everyone, poking into everything, who sets the tone at the Palace. I think I know the one thing he gives above all. It is cheerful, clubby informality. At the Palace, it's all one big, bustling family. I omit the word "happy," because that is a matter for the individual.

I said goodbye to 6,050-foot-high St. Moritz on a February morning amid large flakes of wet snow and pointed my rented Peugeot down-Alps through the Maloja Pass. In less than two hours, cutting across a finger of northern Italy, I traded winter in on a greening, sun-washed springtime. Down to Lugano I came, and at 886 feet found a Switzerland of bright-hued houses with orange-tiled roofs, a Switzerland where olive and chestnut trees grew on enfolding mountainsides and magnolias and mimosa colored the promenade beside a boat-dotted lake. That afternoon a pleasant golf course at nearby Magliaso drew my attention.

On the map, the Ticino, Switzerland's Italian-speaking canton, pushes wedge-like into northern Italy. In a greatly disparate land, no place is more distinctive. "The Swiss-Germans, they are cautious, prudent," a newspaperman said to me. "The French-Swiss, perhaps a bit aloof." He smiled broadly. "But the Italian-Swiss, we are open, friendly. We have the vivacity. We *go!*"

Maybe he overstated the case, but not by much. In all Switzerland, Ticinese grace and animation have no parallel. I can't prove it, but I venture that diet plays a part. In a one-room country restaurant I dined on homemade *salame* and a salad of peppers, soothed my palate with a pungent red wine, and concluded with *formaggino* (goat cheese) and a dollop of throat-clawing *grappa* (white brandy). "You should have put a lump of sugar in it," chided a tablemate, observing my watering eyes.

Sampling such fare, I could savor the élan

of my neighbors—a verve that could sustain itself on porridge and tea. Conversation was rapid, turbulent with smiles and frowns; dark eyes flashed, shoulders shrugged. Later, driving on traffic-thick city streets, it did not surprise me that some cars seemed possessed of demons.

One soon determines that it is good to walk in Lugano on several counts. Its alluring shopping arcades, handsome palazzos, and campaniled Italianate churches deserve to be contemplated at leisure. And nearby, in the little fishing village of Gandria, its old stone houses stacked almost one atop the other along the steep lakeside, I strolled twisting, narrow streets without a care, just as without a care children played in them— Gandria's streets are too small for cars.

At Morcote, another fishing village, I stopped a moment beside the lake where a woman knelt to do her laundry. "You don't see that much any more," my guide remarked, "and not just because the old ways are dying. Lake Lugano . . . the pollution. . . ." He turned up the palms of his hands; he did not like to say it. After we moved on, he brightened. At a construction site, a workman industriously hosed down the mud-encrusted wheels of a huge earth-laden dump truck; it would leave no dirty tracks on Lugano's streets.

The visitor from another land carries away an impression of serene beauty—the lasting image of a glacier-carved blue sapphire of water set in rounded mountains and rimmed with a garden city. Reluctantly I turned my car. In a little while I sighted the roofs and spires of Locarno, an alabaster Swiss city in strong sun, sheltered by benign peaks, nestling in palms against an emerald Lake Maggiore. There I stayed long enough to wonder if Locarno might not be even lovelier than Lugano. I have yet to decide.

Nor could I ever choose between the tiny demicantons of Appenzell—Inner Rhoden and Outer Rhoden. Within their 160 square miles resides the quintessential Switzerland. You expect to meet Heidi here at any moment; and in Johanna Spyri's classic novel that winning lass does live not far away, in the Grisons near the border of Liechtenstein.

These things are Appenzell, and more: plump Brown Swiss cows; wise dogs; beflowered and gaily painted farmhouses with adjoining barns and a common roof; green, manure-redolent highland pastures rolling beneath snowy mountains; festive occasions replete with colorful costumes, yodeling, and harmonizing cowbells; and weather-darkened folk, some of them quite diminutive, clinging stubbornly to the traditions of their ancestors. Here most men and women still wrest their livelihood from the soil. Across the country, just one Swiss in ten works full time at farming.

Switzerland's 25 sovereign "states"—22 full cantons, 3 divided into demicantons—largely practice representative democracy. Only Appenzell and three other cantons still hold the *Landsgemeinde,* the annual open-air assembly where—in direct democracy—laws are made and issues settled by a show of hands. Men carry their swords, symbol of freedom, to the Appenzell Landsgemeinde.

In the town of Appenzell, capital of Inner Rhoden, I learned that sword-carrying interferes with journalist Walter Koller's ability to take notes. "So I put a homemade dagger in my coat pocket," he told me, "and my hands are free for pencil, notebook, and camera."

We sat over coffee in a crowded, paneled restaurant. At the next table, old men played *Jass,* the Swiss national card game; a few women looked on, chatting. I had heard a saying, "Dogs and women must stay home," and I remarked, "I understand that women don't take part in the Landsgemeinde."

Herr Koller laughed. "Not yet!" he said. "But the time shouldn't be too far off."

Now, I should explain that in reality all Switzerland is a patriarchy. Only in 1971 did Swiss women win the right to vote in federal matters; they also have been enfranchised in most cantons, and usually may participate in local issues. But most continue to leave the voting up to their husbands, whether on federal, cantonal, or local levels. In Appenzell's demicantons women as yet have no demicantonal voice. Period.

"Life here follows the dictates of tradition," mused journalist Koller. "Since 1597 Appenzell has been split into two parts. Inner Rhoden is predominantly Catholic, Outer Rhoden Protestant. For a long time there was no mixing of the two. Today the differences show less and less, but all changes come slowly and reluctantly. In 1972 Outer Rhoden gave women the vote in local affairs. Inner Rhoden will decide the issue of full suffrage for women at the next Landsgemeinde."

The large canton of St. Gall completely surrounds Appenzell. This prompts the earthy Appenzeller to quip—"Our land is a gold coin in a sea of dung." In turn, the short

stature of some Appenzellers gives rise to jokes throughout Switzerland, a typical one of which goes: "Why don't they take their annual military training in summer?" "Because they would get lost in the grass."

Between visits to Inner and Outer Rhoden I made my headquarters in busy St. Gall city and relished the contrast. At the new, severely modernistic theater, the musical *Showboat* was playing in high German to a full house of 855. Afterward, in a dimly lit restaurant, I feasted on the tenderest of newly picked asparagus while a pianist worked his way through "Ramona" and "Mexicali Rose." "Unreal," muttered another American beside me. "A delight," said I, and meant it.

At St. Gall's ornate 18th-century Abbey Library I stopped to ponder the Greek inscription over the door: "The Medicine Chest of the Soul." Then I put on felt slippers—protection for the most beautiful parquet floors I shall ever see—and watched scholars at work among 2,000 manuscripts (the oldest from the eighth century), 1,000 books printed before 1501, 100,000 printed later.

I visited the industrial and trades museum, repository of the city's long history as an important textile center. My hostess, Frau Rosmarie Taeschler, lingered beside a stunningly intricate dress of lace and embroidery. "It was made for the Empress Eugenie, Napoleon III's wife," she said. "I wonder if she knew or cared that it took 36 women a year and a half to create it."

SWISS WOMEN, I suppose, have always been handy with needle and thread, of necessity. Until recent times, in remote Alpine villages, they fashioned clothes for themselves and their families. So it has been in the high village of Kippel, in the canton of the Valais. Snow lies deep here from mid-November until May; streams raced with milky glacial melt when I arrived early in June.

The village, population 453, a huddle of weather-blackened chalets and huts, is the largest in the secluded Lötschental—the Lötschen Valley. Above it, in ascending order, stand the hamlets of Wiler, Ried, and Blatten. Beyond Blatten abide only glacial moraine and glacier and alp and sky.

"Our women buy their clothes now," said the Rev. Dr. H. C. Johann Siegen, 86 years old on the day I met him, prior nearly six decades at the Church of St. Martin. "They have it a little easier." We talked in Father Siegen's small sitting room; its immaculate wood floor had been scoured almost white; crucifixes dominated one wall. The stooped, white-haired priest frowned and clasped his hands. "But still, my people work hard. They are born to be hard-working."

Life for the peasant of the Lötschental follows traditional paths. He rises at dawn, labors in the fields all day, goes to bed at 8 p.m. If he can find work in a city, his wife keeps the farm producing. Women marry young, bear many babies rapidly, milk the cows, plant potatoes, help scythe and stack hay, cook, and tend house while their husbands relax in the evenings at the stube.

The train carries you as far as Goppenstein station in the lower Lötschental; not many years ago you walked a mule track from there seven miles to Kippel. Today a paved road ties the high villages to civilization (as do a few television sets), and the postal bus makes scheduled round trips on schedule. I believe that everything in Switzerland runs on schedule, except perhaps for occasional derelictions in the Ticino.

With returning villagers I had caught the up-valley bus from Goppenstein on a sunny Saturday afternoon; on Sunday the high-valley people would celebrate *Segensonntag* (Sunday of Blessing), the colorful festival of Corpus Christi. The bus driver resolutely assured our attendance, sounding his musical horn at every narrow, blind switchback. That clarion call, an inverted triad of bugle notes that open Rossini's *William Tell Overture,* reverberated off steep mountainsides and gave me cold comfort. The shadowy chasms dropping away beneath my window grew no less deep.

In Kippel the weather-worn Pension Bietschhorn made me welcome. Flowering apple trees grew on its terrace and a soft breeze freed white petals. I pushed through the entrance, passed a smoke-filled stube, climbed a creaking stairway to a plain third-floor room with corner washstand, located the bath down the bare-floored hall. No pretensions here—and no need for any, especially at dinnertime: I speared thick, coarse chunks of homemade bread into a rich, tangy cheese fondue until it was impossible to eat more. As dusk fell I dawdled along from one end of the village to another in ten minutes, detained part of the time by the band in earnest concert. That night I slept the sleep of the pure in heart, drugged by sweet Alpine air and the silence of the ages.

Next morning all Kippel turned out in

traditional costumes for the solemn Segensonntag procession: little girls in long white gowns, stalwart men wearing brilliant red uniforms, impassive matrons telling their beads as they filed past in black dresses decorated with gold lace and filigree. Beside me, David McLennan—he and Mrs. McLennan are the only English-speaking residents of the Lötschental—spoke quietly. "This is a world unto itself," he said. "The people keep it that way."

I said, "What about those grenadiers...?"

The entire procession was kneeling now, except for the rifle-bearing soldiers, before a roadside crucifix. "For centuries," he answered, "Swiss men went away to serve in foreign armies—greatest mercenaries in the world. When they made enough money, they came home. Those who returned to the Lötschental and its deeply religious way of life became—as you see—'Grenadiers of God.'"

HERE THE OLD WAYS change slowly, if at all. But now progress, if that be the right term, is coming to the valley, the degree of its impact unknown. "The people want it," said David McLennan. "It is the only way to raise the standard of living."

For nearly a decade, he explained, the English development company he directs has been acquiring land for a large, high-quality resort. "I spent my first six years here buying just 50 acres of land," he said ruefully. "One contract alone required 11 signatures. You need the patience of a saint to deal with the Swiss."

Patience he has. His blueprints reckon the project's cost at one hundred million Swiss francs (about 25 million dollars) and possibly half again more.

I asked to see the development. Up the usual tortuous road we drove, to a high, gently sloping flank. Across the deep valley from us rose the Bietschhorn's snow-glistening peak, topping a wide horizon of white. About us stood a number of large, expensive chalets in various stages of construction.

"This is Lauchernalp," my host announced. "Where you are now is the village square."

I raised an eyebrow. It looked to me like one more marvelous Swiss mountain meadow, a six-inch mat of lush grass dappled with yellow, blue, and purple wildflowers. David McLennan sprawled on that springy carpet, smiled blissfully, and said:

"Ah, I know. You can't envision the waiters in their dinner jackets; you don't hear the clink of gin and tonics. But I can, because it's about 1980 where we are. I see a three-tier village square stepped up the mountainside, surrounded by typical Swiss chalets.

"Beneath the square we shall hide the nightclubs, the entertainment. We'll have a swimming pool, shops, and cinema. Mostly, Lauchernalp will attract skiers; the lifts are going up now. Walkers and hikers also will come. People will live here all year. Mrs. McLennan and I are moving up soon...."

And soon, ineluctably, I was moving down, to Kippel and the postal bus, to Goppenstein where the driver shifted from Swiss-German into French as he shifted into neutral to collect a passenger and her fare—"Bonjour, madame. Merci." How did he know?

Coming into French-speaking Sion, capital and main city of the Canton of the Valais, twenty centuries of life greeted me equably. The eye visits this broad, Alp-cradled valley with calm pleasure. Ancient terraced vineyards climb steeply; Roman legions, tramping by, surely sampled their grapes. The smooth River Rhône idles past the city; Sion itself goes about its business with Gallic insouciance. But I could not be so composed. The heart leaps to see Sion's crowning glories, the majestic ecclesiastical fortresses of Valère and Tourbillon, mounting ancient watch atop high twin promontories. I made my way to them.

Tourbillon, palace of the Bishops of Sion since the 13th century, I found to be a ruin, destroyed by fire in 1788. In silhouette it had seemed vital; closer, it haunted me with the sense of strength it once possessed. Neighboring Valère, I saw, has prospered by comparison, and appears much as it did 700 years ago. It was a fortified cathedral then, abode of canons and seminarians and soldiers; by the late 18th century all had gone. Today, carefully restored, it rings with the shouts of visiting schoolchildren. Many grow thoughtful in the assembly hall as they view the display of shields, swords, crossbows, maces, pikes, halberds, and other items of another day's inhumanity to man.

M. Maurice Wenger, the conservator since 1948, showed me around with obvious affection; his grandfather began here as conservator in 1887, his father in 1913. M. Wenger and his family live in the castle. A musician, he sometimes plays the organ in the cathedral. "This is the oldest playable organ in the world," he said. "It was built in 1390."

A feeling of other-worldliness took hold

of me. For an instant time seemed suspended. "In the night," I asked, "do ghosts come to Valère?"

"*Mais oui.*" The question pleased him. He laughed. "I hear them almost every night," he said. "Always they turn out to be the young lovers."

Many long stone stairways carried me down to Sion's busy streets. I glanced back. Castles should be romantic. *Vive l'amour! Vive Valère!*

To witness another aspect of Switzerland's heritage, I rode a train to Interlaken; dress rehearsals were under way for the annual summer performances of Schiller's stirring drama of Swiss liberation, *William Tell.* In a natural woodland setting on the city's edge, a cast of more than 200, all from the Interlaken area, played out assigned roles with vigor if not, in the trumpeters' instance, with complete fidelity. The story unfolded. As always, the despotic bailiff Gessler, agent of the tyrannical Habsburgs, orders fearless Tell to shoot an apple from his young son's head. When William Tell fires the bolt from his crossbow, the spirit of Swiss independence is reborn.

A different summer spectacle was beginning over in Montreux. On the edge of Lake Geneva, in a hall beneath a casino, the city's Sixth Annual International Festival of Jazz drew cheering listeners both young and old. For 14 days in 15 concerts, musicians from the United States and Europe (including groups from Yugoslavia, Poland, and Hungary) would enliven sedate Montreux.

Above the city, clinging to the side of the mountain named Rochers de Naye, a new superhighway brought new development with it. "Not long ago this land was all farms and vineyards," said M. Raymond Jaussi as we sped up the mountain in his agile Mercedes-Benz. "You'll find few cows here now. New houses eat up the pastures. Tourism replaces the vineyards."

Head of the Montreux Tourist Office and a former Swiss Army officer, Raymond Jaussi took two days out to show me the Switzerland he knows as do few others. Over the Rochers de Naye, we entered the Gruyère region, home of the zesty cheese. I sampled a wedge of it as he drove. "Life changes here also," he noted. "Old men and children used to look after the cattle. Electric fencing does it now. In many parts of Switzerland, about this time of year, you once saw cows on the road, moving up to the high pastures, bells ringing. Today lorries usually carry them up, and bells are decreasing—sometimes tourists steal them. Yodeling will die out one of these days, too."

I wanted to walk through the Great St. Bernard Pass, oldest of the major crossings. Before the birth of Christ, Julius Caesar used a road through this col, linking Rome with transalpine Gaul. For nearly a thousand years monks have maintained a hospice at its highest point, offering weal to impoverished pilgrims, sending out the famed St. Bernard dogs on rescue missions (helicopters with German shepherds have superseded them). In 1800, Napoleon led an army of 40,000 over the Alps here to Marengo, Italy, where he defeated the Austrians.

Snow chokes the crossing about seven months a year—traffic cuts through the Great St. Bernard Tunnel, operational in 1963 as the first automobile tunnel through an Alp. M. Jaussi placed a phone call. Yes, plows had just opened the pass. We drove there, got out, and walked from Switzerland into Italy and back again; large drifts loomed over us and a sharp breeze kept us moving.

For me, it amounted to a kind of quest. Sections of Roman road still exist, and my companion knew where. Just below the monastery we halted, I hoping to watch Roman times, the Middle Ages, and our day come together. I failed: the way of the chariots and legionaries lay beneath snow.

The philosophic Jaussi shrugged. "No matter. Snow melts. The road will still be there whenever you return." And so it will.

THE DURABILITY of the Swiss Confederation itself dates from August 1, 1291, at Rütli, an Alpine meadow above Lake Lucerne. There men of the three forest communities of Uri, Schwyz (whence the name Switzerland), and Unterwalden sealed their "covenant of perpetual alliance." The last cantons—Valais, Neuchâtel, Geneva—joined in 1815.

Exactly a century before Rütli's eternal pact, the fortified town of Bern had been created by Duke Berchtold V of Zähringen, a ruler of Burgundy. Well situated in what would become west-central Switzerland, Bern grew increasingly important as the Middle Ages wore on. In 1848 it became the country's federal seat.

Today, to my way of thinking, no other city possesses Bern's charm. Its Old Town (for Bern's expanding suburbs gleam with new structures) rests in a horseshoe curve of the Aare River, all towers and arcades, red-tiled roofs, fountains and gargoyles and flowers. To while away one's free time strolling in stately Old Town is endless delight.

But Bern's business is government, and that is why I traveled there. The Swiss Parliament elects the seven-man *Bundesrat,* or Federal Council, which exercises executive authority as a body. Its members move up to serve one-year terms as Vice President and then President. In democratic Switzerland the President lives in his own home, rides the streetcar or drives his own automobile, often goes unrecognized. At the Parliament Building I met the next President of the Confederation, M. Roger Bonvin, in his ample and unpretentious office.

An engineer, former mayor of Sion, pilot and mountaineer and cross-country skier, M. Bonvin serves as minister for transport, communications, and energy. One of his aims, he said, is to foster greater appreciation for the role of women: "In our mountains, women have been in charge for a long time —so many men have left the farms for the factory. It is the women who prepare the coming generation."

What might be the coming generation's largest problem, I asked.

He leaned forward, earnestly. "Not to be overtaken by material gain. The soul and spirit of Switzerland should make progress at the same rate as the economy."

I sensed something of that soul and spirit a little later standing before the Zytglog-geturm, or Clock Tower, which once was Bern's west gate. For nearly 450 years the passage of time has been celebrated here as at few other places. The performance began precisely at four minutes before the hour, featuring a cast of moving statues— Father Time and his hourglass, a jaunty merry-go-round of bears, a knight in armor, a jester, a crowing cock, and others.

Afterward I climbed the tower's spiral staircase to see the brains behind this long-running production. A cannonball at least a foot in diameter, the pendulum, swung to and fro. Huge gears turned and clicked. Suddenly—*tic toc tic toc whir click clack clatter*—the entire room seemed in motion. Then I heard the two mellifluous chimes of the half-hour. I would not like to be in that room during the four-minute hourly tableau.

As I left, a small sign caught my eye: *"Alles aufgezogen"*—Everything wound up? In Switzerland, of course it is. □

FOUR A.M. A hint of blue-black dawn east-ward over the sea. Dry dust under a thin veil of Mediterranean mist. The scent of wild mint pungent in the morning air. A lone light in the window of a French farmhouse.

Inside, Adrien Bodrero swallowed the last of his *café au lait,* pulled on his beret, took a well-worn leather whip from a nail in the wall, and slipped out of the door into the twilight. His whip cracked the stillness. A series of whistles and shouts—*"Veni! Veni! Veni!"*—and a gray river of sheep slowly flowed out of the farmyard in a tumult of bells, barking dogs and braying donkeys. His destination: the Alps.

It was a drama repeated over and over each spring, little changed on hundreds of French farms since medieval times. Now it would die.

Little by little the traditional migratory routes of the *transhumance*—the movement of sheep to and from Alpine summer pas-tures—had been replaced by highways, cut by railroads, blocked by cities or dams, choked by ever-increasing traffic. Most sheep-raisers had already turned to train or truck transport. Now, after centuries, the transhumance by foot was doomed.

But once more Adrien Bodrero would make the two weeks' journey. For 29 consecutive years he had taken his sheep 175 miles to pastures in the Alps. A special government permit would enable him to follow the tra-ditional way once again, and he had invited me to accompany him on what might well be his last transhumance.

We left from Fabregas on the Mediter-ranean coast and headed slowly north, pick-ing up other herds of sheep along the way. By the end of the third day, our flock num-bered 1,600 animals. Mules carried supplies. Goats provided milk for dogs or for cheese which we made along the way. Where the route permitted, Adrien's son, Christian, fol-lowed in a van carrying extra supplies and hauling injured or sick animals.

"We used to use a mule cart," Adrien told me, "but the mules died, and the ones we have now were never trained to pull a cart. We bought the van. Already the trans-humance seemed a bit different. But now we have to hire   *(Continued on page 81)*

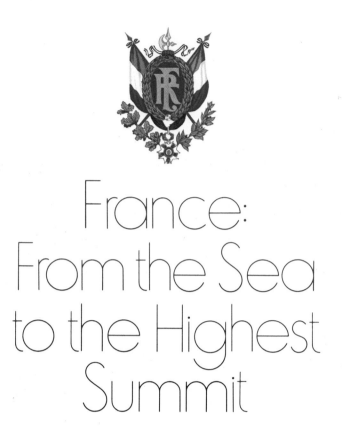

3

France: From the Sea to the Highest Summit

By GEORGE F. MOBLEY
Photographs by the author

Bound for mountain pastures, sheep branded with red dye graze in the foothills of the French Alps at dawn on a misty June day.

Cataract of flame—torches borne by skiers moving together—winds downhill to Val d'Isère; in a 20-minute exposure, stars slash the night sky. On a tour of Mont Blanc glaciers, hikers (above) trudge across the Arête Midi-Plan, an ice-crusted ridge above Chamonix. Straddling a shallow crevasse, a backpacker digs into a hump of ice with his crampons—sharp cleats for use on ice and snow. A rock climber using just the pressure of his body "chimneys" between the granite spikes of the Blades of Planpraz, across the Valley of Chamonix from Mont Blanc.

February snowstorm veils a horse-drawn sleigh near Chamonix. At La Plagne, a sprawling winter-sports complex opened in 1961, a novice skier apprehensively inches forward during her first lesson. A nearby *confiserie* offers freshly baked pastries to skiers coming in hungry from the slopes. With 55 ski runs and nine large hotels, La Plagne bustles with activity; but developers foresee the resort tripling in size—or more—in ten years.

Mist-brimming Valley of Chamonix lies near-ly two miles below a mountaineer scaling the snowy Arête Midi-Plan on the shoulder of Mont Blanc—a peak first climbed in 1786.

Carved by coursing meltwater, an icy grotto plunges into the Mer de Glace—part of the nearly 40 square miles of glacial ice on the flanks of Mont Blanc. Such massive glaciers, often miles in length, form at high elevations receiving heavy snowfall. The pressure of its own weight transforms the snow into ice, and after centuries of accumulation a glacier begins to creep slowly downhill. Above, be-whiskered mountain guide Gabriel "Gabby" Mollard carries equipment essential to gla-cier traverses—an ice ax and safety rope.

Dusky light filters through evening fog over Menton on the Mediterranean coast, where the Maritime Alps rise along the Riviera; within 20 miles they reach heights of more than 9,000 feet. Confetti dapples the flowing muttonchop whiskers of a reveler at Nice's annual Carnaval—a two-week extravaganza preceding Lent. Near Grasse, perfume capital of France, a girl picks fragrant blossoms in a field of lavender; perfumes earn Grasse industries some 84 million dollars a year.

Splattering slush, careering Citroëns crowd perilously close during the Ronde Hivernale, a February race in Chamonix. In a blur of speed, a Porsche rounds a hairpin turn at the 41st Monte Carlo Rallye—one of the most grueling touring-car events; of 264 starters, only 40 completed the 1972 race. The rally consists of three parts: a journey to Monte Carlo by specified routes, a thousand-mile drive on twisting Alpine roads, and a nighttime test of endurance and speed—some 400 miles. In a Porsche 911S, French racer Gérard Larousse nears the finish line to claim second place. Winning driver Sandro Munari of Italy pops a magnum of champagne with his ecstatic navigator Mario Manucci.

Shepherds summering their flocks in high pastures near Mont Blanc relax in the roughhewn Refuge des

Mottets, one of the shelters reserved at night for hikers on the hundred-mile trail that circuits the mountain.

Nibbling grass as they walk, sheep tended by Adrien Bodrero and his dog Falcon move slowly northward to Alpine meadows on a two-week migration—possibly the last in the centuries-old pattern of transhumance; now French sheep-owners must take their flocks to pasture by truck. Climbing a steep path (opposite), the herd of 1,600 approaches journey's end. On a farm nearby, weathered Alphonse Dallé rents mountain pastureland.

Sliver of gold touches a snowy escarpment north of Mont Blanc as dawn breaks over a jagged horizon. Two

alpinists creep upward; a cornice—unsupported snow protruding beyond the rock—soon forced them back.

a truck to take our sheep to the mountains."

We paused a moment, watching the river of wool stream past, listening to the tinkling melody of sheep bells.

"That's music to a shepherd," Adrien said, then sadly added, "and now it's finished. Ça fait mal au cœur—it makes you want to cry. I have a friend who has made the transhumance with me every year for 29 years. This year he sent his sheep by truck. When we left, my wife scolded me for not saying goodbye to him. But I couldn't. He would have wept."

We generally traveled during the cooler hours of the day, stopping when heat became too intense for the sheep. When it cooled enough later in the afternoon, we set out again, usually finishing after dark.

One night we camped near the town of Méounes. In spite of hard ground under my sleeping bag, I fell into an exhausted sleep. Midnight brought wind, scattered drops of rain. I awoke, expecting a downpour. The sheep also sensed a storm and wouldn't settle down, so we packed up and started walking. Numb from sleep, we stumbled on through the night, weaving from one side of the road to the other.

Dawn came, and with it rain. We pushed on, no pasture, no place to sleep. Then at noon we found a rocky field off the road. Too tired to eat, we lay on the rocks, wrapped in our raincoats, and napped for an hour and a half. Then we had bread, sausage, cheese, and wine and again set out to march through intermittent rain until 10 p.m.

"This is a life of misery," commented one of the shepherds, Jean Pierre Levet, "but I love it above all else. For a man to be a good shepherd, the beasts must flow in his blood."

With weary bodies and blistered feet, covered with dust and sweat, we came to the Alps. Vineyard gave way to plateau which gave way to forests and small farms that in turn gave way to rocky cliffs and foaming streams. The heat faded, and we shivered in the cold. The Col d'Allos rose above us; we climbed through snow. Beyond the pass we saw the snow-capped mountains where the sheep would spend the summer.

Adrien walked with pride ahead of his flock, sniffed the mountain air and confided,

Snow burdens the branches of evergreens and a young man scoops clear a driveway, on the day after a 12-inch fall in Chamonix.

"I grew up in the mountains. Every time I return, I feel like I've come home."

When we finally reached the tiny village of St. Paul, friends came out to greet him and offered him wine to celebrate his arrival.

Early the next morning we counted the sheep. One was missing. Adrien looked concerned, then shrugged his shoulders. *"Pas mal.* Not bad, really, after two weeks' walk with 1,600 animals. One year a truck killed 14, and a friend of mine lost a hundred sheep when they were struck by lightning."

He spread salt on rocks for the sheep and made coffee for us. "As summer passes, we will gradually move higher and higher into the mountains along the Italian border. But we will stay here a few days first. The sheep are tired, the dogs are tired, the shepherds are tired. We must rest."

We finished our coffee and, with a sadness known only to people who have shared a moment of their lives together, we said goodbye.

I RETURNED to the sea, this time to the Maritime Alps, that province nestled into the corner where the French-Italian border meets the Mediterranean. Here the Alps rise abruptly from the sea, a giant wave of stone swelling northward to crest in the glacial whitecaps of Mont Blanc.

I had explored much of this province the previous winter. Arriving from Italy via the snowy Col de Tende, I was amazed at an abrupt change in climate as I descended toward the Mediterranean. The road snaked steeply down through stone-walled canyons of the Roya River, past slumbering medieval towns, through olive groves. Along the coast, oranges and lemons clung to green trees. Bougainvillea bloomed everywhere.

I had come south for the Monte Carlo Rallye, and the Principality of Monaco, a tiny enclave in the Maritime Alps, buzzed with excitement, not to mention the roar of cars.

From 25 nations 264 entries had come to this grueling test of car and driver. The tortuous route twists over nearly a thousand miles of Alpine road, snowy passes and hairpin bends. The more I drove it, the more I respected the skills of rally participants, people like Gérard Larousse, Sandro Munari, Timo Makinen, and Björn Waldegaard.

"These men drive by instinct," Chris Sclater, one of the co-drivers, told me. "They have a natural feeling for the car and the road. They push themselves and their cars to the limit, then discover they can go even faster."

Springing from the waters of the Mediterranean, the French Alps sweep northward to the lofty crown of Mont Blanc, then taper away to the Lake of Geneva. Sun-washed hills in the south give way to plunging precipices clad in snow. Riviera resorts and new ski complexes contrast with pastoral villages.

The rally takes place in three stages. First is the assembly at Monte Carlo from countries of departure, by prescribed itinerary from places like Glasgow, Oslo, Warsaw, and Lisbon. Second is a 26-hour endurance test over the mountain route. Finally comes the climax, a frantic all-night trial of sheer speed over a course near Monte Carlo. When this final test was over, only 40 cars remained out of the starting field of 264.

But I had come south to follow a different route. In 1815, when Napoléon escaped from exile on the isle of Elba, he landed at Golfe-Juan, a quiet bay east of Cannes, and began his triumphant march to Paris. He shunned main roads and made his way through the Alps as far as Grenoble. He had triumphed again and again; he had survived calamity in Russia; he had abdicated; now he sought victory again in the drama remembered as the Hundred Days. In 1932, the Route Napoléon was inaugurated. This historic Alpine road follows closely the original route taken by the Emperor in his last adventure.

It is difficult, traveling today by car on pavement, to imagine the hardships faced by Napoléon and his little army on their wintry march. In some places the mountain route was only a rough trail. Carts had to be abandoned and supplies carried by donkeys. Yet, to keep well out of the reach of Royalist forces, Napoléon and his troops covered two hundred miles in six days.

The local population, suspicious and cold in the south, grew more friendly as Napoléon pushed northward until a tumultuous ovation at Grenoble virtually assured the immediate success of his mission, a gamble for power with Royalists of France—and of a wary Europe—allied against him.

At the town of Grasse, where Napoléon left his carts and began the steep climb into the mountains, I stopped for a few days' visit. Napoléon, distrusting the residents, camped outside Grasse; but today it is hard to resist the town. A profuse display of flowers brightens the parks and roadsides, blending their fragrance with the abundant aromas issuing

from the town's leading industry. For Grasse is the perfume capital of France.

From every corner of the globe, hundreds of raw materials pour into Grasse. Some are common, some exotic. Some are exquisite, some vile. Through different processes, aromatic chemicals are extracted, purified and blended into the extremely complex formulas of perfume. These essential oils are in turn exported to perfume producers from New York to Tokyo, from Paris to Rio de Janeiro.

"It began with the tanning industry," explained Pierre Vigne, director of a French producers' association. "Grasse was famous for fine gloves. In the 16th and 17th centuries, perfumed gloves came into fashion in France, and this led to the cultivation of flowers around Grasse. Little by little the leather industry declined, but the perfume industry flourished. Today it's a 400-million-franc-per-year industry in Grasse."

Raw materials are highly varied: fruit rinds, flowers, seeds, roots, bark, mosses, grasses, resins, animal products. Even malodorous civet from the civet "cat" in East Africa serves in minute quantities as a fixative and gives tone to certain perfumes.

The yield is small. "It takes 1,000 kilos of orange blossoms to produce one kilo of *néroli,* a product used in cologne," M. Vigne said. "And jasmine, one of our most prestigious oils, requires 800 kilos to make one kilo of absolute. And it's a very small flower. It takes many flowers to make a kilo."

This is well reflected in the price. One kilo of essential oil from jasmine—2.2 pounds—costs about 20,000 francs ($4,166).

"What does it take to make a truly fine perfume?" I asked.

"An artist," M. Vigne replied. "You must be inspired. But you must also be a chemist."

I visited one of the Grasse firms, P. Robertet & Cie., and talked with one of these artists, English-born Paul E. Johnson.

"Creating a perfume is somewhat like composing music," he said. "With 20 to 40 raw materials, one chooses some for a well-balanced blend, the 'chord' or dominant theme. This chord makes Arpège different from Chanel No. 5 or Shalimar. Added ingredients give warmth or freshness, and so on; they dress up the scent and give it volume."

Johnson and others like him in the industry have earned the title *"le nez,"* the nose. Sometimes "le nez" creates a perfume because he has the urge to create, sometimes to fill a customer's need.

One client, a baker, found sales dropping after he started wrapping his bread in sanitary plastic bags. Investigation revealed that the plastic trapped the delicious odor of fresh bread inside the bag. He asked a Grasse company to develop a perfume that smelled like freshly baked bread, and had this added when the wrappers were manufactured. His sales zoomed back up to normal.

From Grasse, I followed the Route Napoléon to Grenoble. The Emperor went on to Paris; before midsummer he would be at Waterloo. I headed for Savoie, once a duchy strong in its own right, now a province justly renowned for its cheese. Here, countless Alpine farms produce small white cakes of creamy Reblochon.

THE TRADITION of Reblochon dates from the Middle Ages, when the feudal lords of the area imposed a heavy tax—payable in milk—on each cow. So severe was the tax that little milk was left for the farm family.

In an effort to save something for themselves, farmers started partially milking their cows. Then, after the milk had been picked up for their overlords, they secretly completed the task. They used this milk, extra rich in fat content, to make into cheese which they called Reblochon. The name, in the local dialect, means "second milking."

To see Reblochon produced, I drove up the side of a mountain to the end of a cow path—the farmer insisted it was quite adequate for his jeep—and visited for a couple of days with Marcel Burnier and his family. The farm sits high in an Alpine valley where an abundance of sweet summer grass assures a good supply of milk. In winter he moves the cows down to the village of Entremont.

Ten milch cows are adequate here to provide a comfortable living, though most small Alpine farms in France are beginning to feel the competition from large commercial producers. The Burniers work together, a little son holding (and petting) a goat while his father milks it, an older daughter efficiently sharing her mother's chores.

Heating the fresh milk requires precise temperature and timing. Once the milk is "set" and curdled with rennet, Mme Burnier strains the curds and packs them into molds where iron weights press out the whey. After several hours, the cakes are removed from the molds and placed on shelves to dry.

Twice a day the animals are milked, twice a day cheese is made. The Burniers produce not only Reblochon but also large wheels of mild Tomme de Savoie and tiny cakes of Chevrotin, salt-tinged and pungent goat cheese. Reblochon ages four weeks, the others longer, in the cellar below the farmhouse, where an earth floor gives musty weight to the still, dark air of the *cave*.

I slept in the hayloft that night and went out early next morning to help M. Burnier bring in the cows. Then, with a good supply of cheese in my car, I headed for Chamonix and the sovereign of the Alps, Mont Blanc.

Chamonix, one of the earliest resorts in the French Alps, was well known long before the formal opening of the Mont Blanc Tunnel in 1965 placed it on the most direct route—the "White Way"—from Paris to Rome.

Construction crews started at both sides of the massif, near Chamonix on French soil and a hamlet at the upper end of the Valle d'Aosta in Italy. For four years they burrowed on this 7.2-mile-long tube of stone, sometimes working under 1.5 miles of Alpine glacier and rock. Drilling into relatively dry and stable rock, gneiss and schist and granite, the French team used heavy, electrified equipment. In zones of crumbling slaty phyllite or marly schists, the Italian miners had to resort to pick and shovel; they reached good rock only after three years, and then for a limited distance. When the teams met in the center of the mountain's granitic core, they were off by 5.3 inches in axis, 8.3 inches in level at the junction.

"When a charge of dynamite smashed the final wall of stone separating the two sections, the engineer wept," a Chamonix friend told me. "He saw the moment as a symbolic reunion of two great Latin peoples."

But the price in toil and lives was high: 17 men died on the project, and a historian has noted that "chances of getting hurt came uncomfortably close to certainty."

Not the engineering feat, marvelous as it was, attracted me to Mont Blanc so much as the lofty mass of stone, snow, and ice itself.

From the moment I first saw Mont Blanc, I felt the attraction which has drawn so many to explore her glaciers, scale her walls of granite, and ultimately stand on her summit. But I had to be in better condition. First, I would walk around Mont Blanc.

The Mont Blanc massif sprawls over 1,670 square miles in France, Italy, and Switzerland. Alpine clubs in the three countries maintain a 100-mile trail around the massif, plus various alternate routes and a host of other trails. They have also constructed refuges in more isolated areas where hikers and mountaineers can find shelter and food.

I joined a group of hikers from Chamonix. With rucksacks laden with extra clothing, food, a tent, maps, guidebooks, and photographic equipment, we set out in a counterclockwise direction around the mountain.

The route alternated between windswept passes and warm, green valleys. Often we saw flocks of sheep or herds of cows which had come to Alpine slopes for the summer. And always, to our left, rose the rugged cliffs and enchanting glaciers of Mont Blanc.

We crossed into Italy at Col de la Seigne. No passport facilities, no customs officials, only a cairn of stone and the wind. Our passage into Switzerland was just as easy.

For a week we slept in isolated refuges or tiny mountain village inns or camped beside clear mountain lakes. One rainy night we slept in the hayloft of a mule stable while the pewter sky over our heads cracked with fissures of blue lightning.

At Arpette, our last stop before returning to France, we dined on raclette, a Swiss specialty of melted cheese served with boiled potatoes. A Belgian boys choir and their escorts were staying in the same hotel, and everywhere there was music. A young woman played Beethoven, Mozart, and Chopin's "Valse de l'adieu" on the piano. A guitar appeared, and we sang folk songs in French, English, and Flemish. Gérard Bisson, one of my companions, took the guitar and we all danced "La Bamba."

In the morning, the boys gave us an impromptu concert during breakfast, finishing with "Carry Me Back to Old Virginny."

It was a long, hard climb through the foggy Fenêtre d'Arpette, most rugged pass on the Tour du Mont Blanc. Spring flowers, clinging precariously to the rock slopes, peeked timidly through a carpet of fresh snow. We descended deep into another valley, stopped for lunch at a tiny refuge, and climbed our final pass, the Col de Balme, back into France.

"It was through this pass," Gérard reminded me, "that French guides smuggled Jews out of German-occupied territory into neutral Switzerland during the war."

My tour of Mont Blanc was finished, but my walking was not. The next day, I met two young Chamonix guides, Joseph Bellin and Pierre Ravanel. We were going to explore the Mer de Glace. This, France's biggest glacier, is formed by several glaciers that flow and tumble slowly down from their birthplace, the perpetual snowfields high within the massif.

I wanted to follow the glacier downward from the top, so we took the téléphérique from Chamonix to l'Aiguille du Midi, a spectacular ride which climbs 9,226 feet from the valley floor to this 12,605-foot-high pinnacle of granite. From here, other spidery cables carry their four-place aluminum télécabines 3.16 miles out over the Vallée Blanche and Glacier du Géant to the Italian frontier, where another series of téléphériques descends to La Palud near Courmayeur. All told, it forms Europe's loftiest aerial cableway.

We left the téléphérique at l'Aiguille du Midi and hiked an hour across snow to Cosmic Refuge, popular name for a mountaintop laboratory of the Centre National de la Recherche Scientifique. The laboratory was built for the study of cosmic rays but now is used primarily by glaciologists.

WE WATCHED evening shadows slowly grow longer until the sun finally sank over the horizon. There were mountains in the distance far below us, ships of stone on a silent sea of gray fog. Next morning we had already walked far before the sun reappeared.

"Which route do you want to take?" Joseph asked, "the Arête Midi-Plan?"

"C'est parfait—perfect," I replied, not knowing one route from another.

Joseph clamped a rope to a belt around my waist and we buckled on our crampons, those metal spikes mountaineers use to get a grip on sloping ice. Then I learned exactly what the Arête Midi-Plan was: the steeply undulating edge of a giant blade of ice and snow with the crevassed glacial surface of Vallée Blanche far below to the right and Chamonix 1.75 miles below to the left.

"Come on, it's not hard," Joseph encouraged me as we crawled up a wall of icy granite. I looked at the space beneath my feet and wondered what madness had driven me where not even eagles venture.

Finally we found a flat rock big enough to hold the three of us and gulped down a snack of bread, cheese, bacon, and cold tea. The first cable car had arrived from Chamonix, and a group of climbers crept along the ridge leading away from l'Aiguille du Midi like ants slowly crawling down the edge of a knife.

After eating, we slipped down the granite wall and started a steep descent across a snow-covered glacier. Joseph and Pierre picked a winding course, always alert for

Suspended between cloud and sunlight, backpackers on the Tour du Mont Blanc *— a three-country trail encircling the mountain — descend from the 8,316-foot-high Grand Col Ferret, a pass between Italy and Switzerland.*

danger. Sons and grandsons of Chamonix guides, both were graduates of the national school of *alpinisme* and members of the prestigious Compagnie des Guides de Chamonix. A lifetime here had tempered their love for the mountains with respect.

Morning sun softened the snow. Walking became difficult. Suddenly I felt the snow let go under my foot. Instantly the rope was taut. Slowly I struggled back to solid snow and then peered into the hole I had made. Under a bridge of soft snow yawned a broad crevasse, its aqua colors fading into a deep blue-green darkness.

"Now you see why we're roped together," said Joseph. "Lower on the glacier where the snow cover has melted, you can see the crevasses. But up here the snow doesn't melt, and it very often hides the danger.

"Sometimes the snow holds and forms a bridge that you can cross safely."

"And sometimes it doesn't," Pierre added, "This is one of the greatest dangers in walking on glaciers, and it's especially bad when the snow gets soft — like it is now."

We moved on.

"Attention!"

The shouted warning came from above. I looked up to see a rock plummeting toward us, but it smashed into a boulder lodged in the ice and sank harmlessly into soft snow.

"And that's why we start so early in the morning," Joseph said. "People who know the mountains rarely go out in the afternoon. They go before thawing ice releases rocks or avalanches. But walk now, talk later."

We fairly raced across a couloir where scattered rocks and furrowed snow gave evidence of danger from above. Shortly after noon we reached the Refuge du Requin, removed our packs and shoes, ate, and sprawled in the sun to rest.

From the edge of the cliff where we perched, we looked out over an ice fall called Séracs du Géant and the Glacier du Tacul which joined the Glacier de Leschaux to form the massive Mer de Glace, Sea of Ice.

Like all Alpine glaciers, the one below us formed at high altitudes where annual snow accumulation exceeds evaporation. Over centuries, the snow is compacted into ice and under the pressure of its own weight it begins to flow downhill as a river of ice. At sharp changes or a sharp drop in its course, the glacier cracks open in the huge fissures called crevasses. If the drop is steep enough, it may further break up into the huge blocks of unstable ice called séracs.

Night fell again over the mountains, and safe inside the refuge we talked by the pale light of gas lanterns until bedtime. Abruptly the door banged open. A shaken climber stumbled in from the dark, mumbling something about a companion in a crevasse and the need of light.

We found the climber's exhausted colleagues, the group we had watched that morning on the ridge from l'Aiguille du Midi, approaching the refuge in the dark helping the injured man. Saved from a serious fall by his rope, he had badly twisted one knee. Next morning the rescue helicopter of the Gendarmerie from Chamonix would pick him up and carry him to the hospital for treatment.

"It's a wonder there aren't four times as many accidents as there are," Joseph said. "Most of that group were complete novices, never been in the mountains before; no guide and no lights. They're lucky they made it."

The next morning we explored the Séracs du Géant and picked our way around crevasses on the Mer de Glace. From its lower end, we took a cog railway back to Chamonix.

At last I felt ready. The tour of Mont Blanc had gotten me in shape, and exploring glaciers had helped me acclimatize a bit.

After a good night's sleep at Chamonix, Joseph, Pierre, and I headed for the summit.

Through swirling mist and falling snow we climbed a precipitous rocky ridge to the Refuge de l'Aiguille du Goûter. The refuge seemed an international gathering place for climbers ready for the final assault. There were Japanese, Austrians, Germans, French, Swiss, British, and members of a mountaineering club from Guadalajara, Mexico.

Snow fell and wind howled around the refuge throughout the night. I slept fitfully, fearful the storm would thwart us. Then I was awakened by silence.

THREE A.M. Pale starlight on a sea of clouds. Wind-sculptured ice under six inches of fresh snow. The biting tang of zero degrees. Three tiny figures crawl up the spine of a frozen giant. Wind comes again. Ice particles hiss around our boots and fall off into space. Starlight fades into dawn. Sunrise caresses the snow.

Step by slow step we climb ever upward, heart throbbing, head aching, past cliffs of ice, past a jagged chunk of metal which juts from the snow like a frozen monument to some forgotten world. It is the last evidence of an Air India Constellation which slammed into Mont Blanc in 1950; the rest lies deep within the ice.

Gradually the slope eases and spreads out, and at last there is no more. Only sky remains above us; below us the Alps march off to the horizon. At 15,771 feet we stand on the summit of Mont Blanc, highest of the Alps, the crown of Western Europe.

I drop my rucksack into the snow and sit beside it, filled with awe by the panorama around us. I think of the first men to see this view, Dr. Michel Paccard and Jacques Balmat, Chamoniards who conquered Mont Blanc in 1786; and I visualize the mountaineers who have labored to the summit since. And in the shadowy forms of glaciers far below, my fantasy traces the frozen procession of souls who perished in the attempt, climbers swept away by avalanches, crushed by falling ice, overcome by storms.

Slowly exhaustion gives way to exhilaration, and I understand.

I want to linger on the summit, to savor the sun and wind and cold a bit longer. But we plan to traverse the massif, and at lower elevations the snow will soon grow soft. Reluctantly, we shoulder our rucksacks and begin the long walk down. □

RAIN CLOUDS hung like a half-lifted stage curtain across the Rhine Valley the morning I made my way to the castle on the cliff above Vaduz. *"Grüss Gott,"* said the smiling watchman as he checked my credentials at the gate. "God's blessings on you."

My shoes crunched on the combed gravel drive as I accompanied Walter Kranz, Chief of Protocol for the Principality of Liechtenstein, toward a meeting with His Serene Highness Prince Franz Josef II.

Over an ancient drawbridge we strode, through an inner gate, into a cobbled courtyard. Lanterns nodded overhead. A blackfrocked figure, the castle chaplain, materialized out of the mist to murmur a greeting.

Suddenly the medieval spell was shattered. The planks of the drawbridge stuttered beneath the weight of a tangerine-colored Morris Mini that varoomed past us. Out stepped Princess Marie, stylishly clad and attractive, the young wife of Crown Prince Hans Adam, on her way to pay a call on her mother-in-law. She threw us a smile and disappeared into the castle.

So it is in Liechtenstein. The 13th century, I found, often rubs shoulders with the 20th. In the three weeks I spent exploring this mountain-ringed principality with my wife, Marge, I observed many such giant-sized generation gaps. For Liechtenstein has built a modern economy on the foundations of a history that made it the last remnant of the Holy Roman Empire.

In earlier times, the country's location on a main route through the Alps invited invasion by Roman legions, Charlemagne, and Napoleon. Today the invaders are summer tourists. Exports from new industrial plants flow across the Rhine into next-door Switzerland, into Austria to the east, West Germany to the north, and Italy to the south. In a single generation, Liechtenstein has evolved from an agricultural to an industrial state.

That this small, independent country exists at all seemed to me a political and economic miracle. How has Liechtenstein, with no army of its own to defend its 61 square miles, had the good fortune to remain unconquered? I asked Prince Franz Josef as we sat talking in his paneled study among reminders of his (Continued on page 97)

4

Liechtenstein: Last Remnant of an Empire

By Arthur P. Miller, Jr.
Photographs by Walter Meayers Edwards

Arms and armor of a princely house linked with Austria's rest on the flag of a state economically Swiss and politically unique.

"On the banks of the young Rhine lies Liechtenstein, resting on Alpine heights," proclaims the national anthem. Fed by meltwater from spring thaws, the river threatens to flood the fertile valley and its cities—southernmost Balzers (the nearest in the view at right), Triesen, Vaduz, capital and home of Their Serene Highnesses Princess Georgina and Prince Franz Josef II, twelfth sovereign of his line but the first to take up permanent residence here.

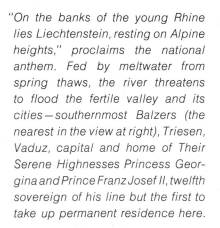

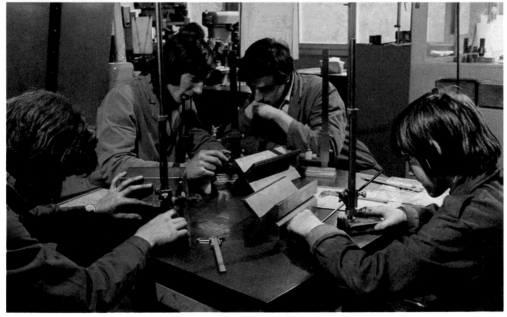

Artist, archeologist, legislator, Dr. Georg Malin displays some of his contributions to postage-stamp art and the national coffers. Stamp sales, a three-million-dollar business, account for 25 percent of Liechtenstein's revenue. At Vaduz (top), sidewalk vending machines dispense the principality's best-selling souvenir—canceled stamps. In the last 30 years, the economy bounded from agrarian to industrial, creating an acute shortage of labor. To expand the work force, firms recruit one out of every four employees from abroad, mainly from neighboring Austria, and conduct vocational training programs. At a Balzers plant, teen-age apprentices (above) prepare for jobs in engineering.

Fireworks over Castle Vaduz end the August 15th celebration of the Prince's birthday, officially advanced

a day to coincide with the Feast of the Assumption, a public holiday in this predominantly Catholic land.

forebears. Last of the reigning Habsburgs, the prince is a grandnephew of Archduke Franz Ferdinand of Austria whose assassination touched off World War I.

"We have indeed been lucky," he responded. "History has been kind to us." Outside, rain trickled down leaded glass windows as he traced his country's past.

It was in 1712 that the prosperous Liechtenstein family of Austria purchased from a bankrupt lord the second of two parcels of land that together form the country.

In 1719, Emperor Karl VI issued letters patent elevating the fiefs to be the Principality of Liechtenstein. The family hardly needed land—Liechtensteins already owned rich estates in Central Europe. But by buying this small Alpine domain, Prince Johann Adam gained a voting seat in the Council of the Princes, the consultative assembly of the Holy Roman Empire.

Typically, luck played a hand in 1806 when the principality gained its independence. Napoleon, conqueror of the Holy Roman Empire, did a favor for a defeated but respected foe, Prince Johann I of Liechtenstein, the Austrian commander-in-chief. Napoleon ordered that the principality be brought into the new confederation of the Rhine as a full member.

"Napoleon was friendly toward my great-great-grandfather," the Prince told me, "but the friendship went in one direction only." Six years later, Prince Johann helped defeat Napoleon. Liechtenstein, of course, retained its now won sovereignty.

When Count Otto von Bismarck unified Germany, the Iron Chancellor picked up all the pieces except little Liechtenstein, which was quietly blending into the Alpine scenery. By the end of World War I, Liechtenstein found itself with all the independence it could use—but not much else. Gone was the imperial glitter of Austria-Hungary. Another Prince Johann, Johann II, mortgaged the family's art collection to buy food for his starving countrymen.

Adrift in international seas, Liechtenstein turned westward to forge ties with Switzerland that still hold today. Under these agreements the Swiss collect duties at the Liechtenstein border, represent the principality

In mid-June, flowers blanket a pasture above Triesenberg. The Alpine hut stores hay and provides shelter for cattle during the winter.

abroad, and run its postal, telephone, and telegraph systems. In return, the 22,000 Liechtensteiners use the stable Swiss currency, take jobs if they choose in Switzerland, and trade freely across the Rhine.

This link with Switzerland, the Prince pointed out, probably preserved Liechtenstein's neutrality during World War II. Hitler never attacked Liechtenstein or its economic partner, Switzerland—which backed its neutrality with a well-drilled army and air force.

By keeping his small country neutral, Prince Franz Josef also achieved a private triumph. He saved the art collection—the most valuable in the world still in private hands. I heard estimates of its worth as high as 150 million dollars. Several of these paintings looked down on us as we toured the halls and armory of this lived-in castle. Most of the treasure of 1,500 paintings, 75 tapestries, and antique silver remains out of sight, stored deep in the former wine cellar. "Everything stays under constant temperature and humidity control," Chief of Protocol Kranz informed me. "It takes much care."

FOR THOSE who cannot view the princely paintings firsthand, collecting Liechtenstein's handsome postage stamps is the next best thing. Many of the hidden old masters appear on the principality's stamps.

The first-day sale of a new stamp issue is a busy time for Hugo Meier, director of the *Postwertzeichenstelle,* the Official Philatelic Service. On this June day I found the energetic chief behind his desk answering last-minute telephone inquiries.

"We have 100,000 standing orders for each of 20 new stamps we issue each year," he explained. He gestured toward a world map prickled with pins. "Orders come from 70 countries. For this issue, which pictures our towns of Vaduz and Bendern, we are also filling 20,000 individual requests."

Between phone calls, Herr Meier explained that his country resists making too much of a good thing. "Some countries raise the face value of each new stamp," he said with a frown. "We keep ours low—14 Swiss francs, four dollars total face value for the 20 new stamps this year. That way we don't discourage sales by making stamp collecting too expensive."

When the snow melts on the lower slopes and the southerly *Föhn* wind warms the valley, tourists flock to Liechtenstein like migrating birds. As Marge and I strolled the

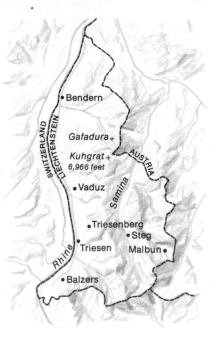

Bordered by the Rhine and by the Rhaetian Alps, Liechtenstein lies at the crossroads of Munich-Milan and Basel-Vienna traffic.

streets of Vaduz at midday, we usually counted a dozen or more big-windowed buses parked in front of the shops. Tour directors were making good on their promise to "see ten countries in 17 days."

Once I wandered into a souvenir shop at the height of the noontide shopping ritual. Two ample American matrons eyed a seemingly endless row of small steins, each with the Liechtenstein crest imprinted upon it.

Visibly perplexed, one asked: "Where's Liechtenstein?"

"You're in it, dear."

Visitors who treat Liechtenstein as a lunch-stop miss much of its flavor: a hike along a sweet-scented Alpine trail; quiet hours fishing in a canal; a swoop in a chairlift to an 8,000-foot view at Malbun; luncheon at a restaurant in a vineyard to savor the local red Vaduzer wine and admire the huge 300-year-old *Torkel* that squeezed the grapes. We enjoyed all these.

But few big winepresses remain, and old ways fade. "Only 3 percent of our people today make their living at agriculture." Dr. Alfred Hilbe, Liechtenstein's tall, lean head of government, defined his country's dramatic turnabout as we talked in his sunny office. "Scarcely a generation ago we were a nation of small farmers and tradesmen."

Then a man with ten milch cows and a garden full of vegetables had almost all he needed; and farmer Adolf Schaedler and his wife, who live high on the slopes at Triesenberg, gave me a glimpse of this passing rural scene as they spoke of dwindling herds in the Samina Valley around Steg.

Would his son follow him into cattle raising? "He's thinking of it," said Herr Schaedler. "But he sees the money others make in the factory, so I don't know."

Failure of farm boys to follow in their fathers' footsteps concerns William Hoop, Minister of Agriculture and Forestry. "If we don't cultivate Alpine fields we may bring more avalanches." I must have looked puzzled. "Let me explain. If no one cuts the hay in a high, sloping field, the grass grows tall. When heavy snows come, the tall grass bends beneath it to form a slick carpet that invites a slide. Cut the grass and the short spikes stick up to hold the snowfall."

In 1967, a citizens committee on erosion swung into action. I saw some results: steel beams to intercept snowslides, fresh plantings of evergreens. "With more and more people coming to see our Alps," Herr Hoop said, "we must take measures now or it will be too late."

Saving the Alps is important to industrialists too—their workers head for the hills on weekends. In Liechtenstein, the industrial revolution arrived late, after World War II. But it came speedily, seemingly painlessly. Businessmen profited from the industrial birth pangs in other nations to create a capitalism with built-in social security programs and little labor turmoil. One sure sign of prosperity: Cars outnumber cattle.

"The strength of the boom surprised most of us," Dr. Hilbe had told me. Once, young Liechtensteiners looked elsewhere for jobs; now 25 percent of the country's work force are foreigners.

Income and corporation taxes, I found, rank among the lowest in Europe. Similarly, the government levies light taxes on holding companies that transact no business in Liechtenstein but deposit their assets there. Result? An estimated 20,000 such companies have set up shop in what I heard called "the Delaware of Europe."

With few raw materials of its own, Liechtenstein specializes in light industry to produce sophisticated products. Martin Hilti, president of his firm, enthusiastically described how Hilti fastening systems used in building construction are sold worldwide. At Balzers AG, youthful Josef Sele led me past high-vacuum chambers where technicians applied thin coatings to lenses and instruments, including the solar wind gauge that Apollo 16 astronauts carried to the moon.

While Balzers exports Space Age hardware, other Liechtensteiners export knowhow and goodwill. To my surprise, I discovered that Liechtenstein has its own peace corps. Its Development Service was founded in 1965 in memory of President John F. Kennedy, originator of the U. S. Peace Corps. In its first eight years, the Development Service sent eleven volunteers to seven countries: among them, a carpenter to Tanzania, a stonemason to Malawi, an architect and his teacher wife to Indonesia.

"Small countries like ours have special feeling for other small nations," said Dr. Gerard Batliner, a former head of government who originated the Development Service. "And being recently industrialized, we know what it's like to be underdeveloped."

I sought out its first volunteer, brown-haired Ingrid Batliner (no relation to the former head of government). Ingrid recounted how she served as a nurse, first in Algeria, later in Tanzania. She displayed the same compassion mixed with culture shock I had seen in Peace Corps returnees. "Back here we have so much. In Tanzania, people are starving. Here everyone has diet problems."

Our stay in Liechtenstein was nearing its end. But I had yet to hike the Furstensteig, the "Prince's Pathway," a mile-high trail that traces a ridgeline of the Rhaetian Alps along the Rhine. "Too early," I was warned. "Snow's still up there. It might be dangerous." Our new Alpine boots, barely broken in, waited in the closet.

Finally, a bit of Liechtenstein luck rubbed off. The weather turned balmy. Accompanied by a guide, Artur Buchel, an off-duty policeman with a ready smile, we set out for the heights. Bit by bit, Artur shared his mountaineering experience: Walk slowly and steadily to pace yourself; let each boot swing like a pendulum as you stride; on a rock face, prove each handhold and foothold.

At Kuhgrat, 6,966 feet, highest point on the trail, we feasted on sandwiches and fruit as we took in the widescreen view of Austria, Switzerland, and Liechtenstein. Black *Bergdohle* birds wheeled through the air below us. Down the slope a *Schneehuhn,* or ptarmigan, croaked a mating cry. A cumulus cloud caught on a peak of the Drei Schwestern, the Three Sisters, shredding into cotton wisps. The peaks, as Artur told it, take their name from three sisters who were turned to stone when they refused to share fresh-picked strawberries with the Virgin Mother.

By midafternoon we descended toward Gafadura. My toes tried to push out the front of my boots, but at trail's end near-vertical leveled to horizontal as we crossed a meadow painted by the late sun's golden glow. At the Gafadura Hutte, genial Frau Emil Fries awaited aching hikers. After serving *Bier,* she insisted we sign her guest book.

Had any of the signers hiked the length of the Furstensteig this season? *"Nein,* the trail it is not yet officially open."

"We have just opened it," I reported with a smile, trying to sound as casual as any veteran mountaineer. I sank contentedly into my chair, reflecting that in Liechtenstein everyone can feel like a prince. □

5

PARALYZED BY THE WEIGHT of snow, I resist the urge to struggle and try to concentrate on Hans Ettl's advice: "If you are trapped in an avalanche, lie still and breathe lightly—you can survive for as long as two hours if you don't panic."

There is, I remind myself, no reason to panic, for Hans has buried me here himself, in order to prove a point—that a well-trained dog can locate avalanche victims more quickly than any modern electronic device. In this case the dog is Hans' four-year-old female German shepherd named Blanka, and I am the volunteer victim.

Now, as the cold begins to seep through my parka, I have misgivings. Hans has buried me three feet down in the remains of a recent avalanche, arranging me with a small air chamber at my head. Then he has piled snow back on top of me, shutting out all but a faint aura of light, and camouflaged the spot.

It occurs to me belatedly that if Blanka fails the test, I have no assurance Hans himself can locate me. Moreover, in wet snow, three feet is below the level at which I can dig myself out. I am thoroughly trapped, and if the avalanche begins to shift again I am in very serious trouble.

I long for a look at my watch, but there is not enough light. How many minutes have I been here—perhaps thirty? And how many more until my air begins to give out? Surely Blanka is long overdue....

A sudden vibration interrupts my thoughts, and for one terrible moment I am sure the avalanche is moving. Then a blob of snow lands on my cheek and there is an insistent scratching overhead. More blobs, and a fissure of light streaks the gloom above me. The fissure widens, and suddenly there is Blanka's face, only inches from mine. For a long moment we stare at each other, and I have an absurd notion she is smiling.

Certainly Hans is smiling, his rugged Bavarian face aglow as he helps me out of my temporary tomb. I realize the reason when I glance at my watch—Blanka has found me in approximately three minutes.

"With a *Magnetmeldegerät*," Hans says, using the German word for a metal detector, "one must sweep a huge area inch-by-inch, whereas Blanka" *(Continued on page 113)*

Bavaria: Proud People and Harsh Beauty

By WILLIAM GRAVES
Photographs by GEORGE F. MOBLEY

Pilgrimage shrine for the mountain folk, the little baroque chapel in the valley village of Maria Gern awaits an impending blizzard.

Amid flying powder snow, the expert's favorite, a skier traverses the spruce-forested Tegelberg. This area, not far from the village of Hohenschwangau, offers winter sports and summer hiking as well as many picturesque castles; in the 19th century Bavarian royalty built homes in this region out of fondness for its scenery and its placid rural ways. Even today life for the farmer has not changed greatly here — horses may still draw a covered wagon on a lonely gray-white lane. Late-October ice encrusts the last wildflowers of summer near a highland lake's snowy edge.

Commanding a view of the bluish-green Alp-See, girdled by dark forests, King Ludwig's fairy-tale marble castle Neuschwanstein rises from a lofty rock west of Hohenschwangau.

—he gives her a rough pat—"can pick up the scent 50 yards away, even when the victim is buried as much as 12 feet down. At that depth, the average detector is useless."

He glances toward the pit and then at Blanka once more. "Sometimes, the old ways are still the best."

In a sense, Hans speaks for all Bavarians, or at least for those who inhabit the high Alps. Born in a harsh but beautiful land, trained early to independence and respect for the past, the Alpine Bavarians are slow to change, clinging to traditions handed down over the long reach of centuries.

Pride, too, runs deep among the mountain folk. No true Alpine villager ever refers to himself simply as a Bavarian, but always as an *Oberbayer,* an Upper Bavarian. The distinction is real, for the great majority of Bavarians (some 85 percent) are lowlanders— or, as the mountain people put it, with more sympathy than scorn, *Plattfuss Indianern* ("Flatfoot Indians").

As a Flatfoot Indian of the American variety, I confess the Alpine Bavarians have a point: theirs is the most beautiful and varied region of all Germany.

Statistically, the Bavarian range is of minor rank. Its highest mountain, the Zugspitze, rises a mere 9,721 feet—more than a mile short of Mont Blanc. In area the range measures only 800 square miles—roughly one percent of the entire Alpine region, but a spectacular one percent.

I began my tour of Upper Bavaria in late winter, via that magnificent gateway to the Alps, the city of Munich. Third largest of West Germany's metropolitan centers, with nearly 1,500,000 residents, Munich lies near the southern edge of the broad Bavarian plain, some 50 miles north of the Alps.

Few cities are more gifted at the art of welcome, for Munich specializes in *Gemütlichkeit,* a nearly untranslatable word combining touches of hospitality, ease, and good fellowship. Amply equipped with restaurants, beer gardens, and wine cellars, the capital of Bavaria exudes an air of relaxed charm.

Munich serves as a giant base camp for the Bavarian Alps, sheltering visitors before their ascent. While the city manages to accommodate the growing number of transients,

Scanning the jagged gray gorge and shifting clouds below, a hiker pauses on a snow-dusted crag near Garmisch-Partenkirchen.

the Alps are hard put to absorb them. From a relative handful who visited the Alps in the period following World War II, the human tide has swollen to more than 5,000,000 vacationers a year.

Faced with invasion on such a scale, the Bavarian Government has taken steps to preserve the natural character of the Alps. In June 1971, the state authorities adopted a comprehensive *Alpenraumplan,* or "Alpine Space Plan." At the Ministry of Environmental Protection in Munich, staff assistant Hans Neumeyer outlined it for me on a map shaded in red, yellow, and green.

"Fortunately," Herr Neumeyer began, "the State Government owns nearly half of all the land in our Alps, so that much of the area is already in reserve. The portions you see marked in red, nearly 40 percent, will be maintained as wilderness. The yellow areas, another 40 percent, are set aside for commercial development—winter sports centers, hotels, and light industry. The remaining 20 percent, shown in green, will be essentially natural land with strictly limited development."

It seemed a well-balanced plan and I asked how the Alpine people themselves viewed it.

"The great majority are in favor of it," Herr Neumeyer answered. "Land, after all, is their most precious asset; many tracts have been passed down through the same family for more than five centuries. The Bavarians have seen what overdevelopment can do. They want no part of it in the Alps."

CERTAINLY Anderl Heckmair would subscribe to that view, although his favorite portions of the Alps are hardly in danger. I met Anderl and his charming wife, Trudy, in the small town of Oberstdorf, the first stop on my west-to-east route.

Oberstdorf lies near the border with Austria, in the region known as Allgäu. Motoring south and west from Munich, I entered Allgäu by way of the broad Iller Valley, driven like an enormous green wedge into the limestone mass of the Allgäu Alps.

Nothing quite prepares a visitor for that first view of the Alps. In the distance they rise from the green plains like some monstrous typhoon, forever gathering above a tranquil sea. Viewed close at hand, they soar impossibly high, from bases embroidered by forests of spruce and pine to distant peaks enameled most of the year by snow.

Like many another Alpine community,

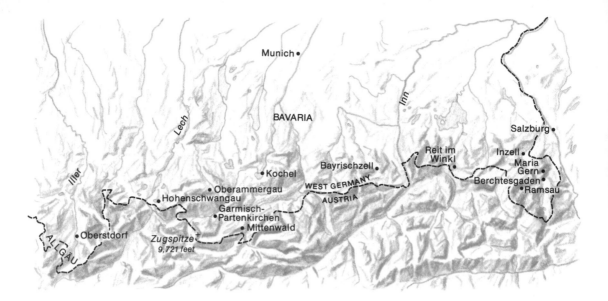

Bavaria's Alps, roughly one percent of the entire range, stretch along the Austrian border from near Salzburg in the east to Lindau on the Boden See in the west. Although this area boasts no exceptionally high or famous mountains, it does claim Germany's loftiest peak, the 9,721-foot-high Zugspitze.

Oberstdorf cheerfully ignores national boundaries, freely borrowing customs and traditions from Austria, Switzerland, and France. Lodged in a cleft of the great Allgäu range, the town huddles close to narrow cobbled streets whose shops display "French" pastries, Tyrolean wear, and bronze cowbells in the style of Switzerland.

In other respects Oberstdorf is pure Allgäu, with its rugged independence, its quiet charm and instinctive hospitality. It is no accident that the town's symbolic mascot is the *Wilde Männle,* or "Little Wild Man," a puckish figure from prehistoric Celtic times, always pictured in a coarse smock of woven lichen and noted for his love of dancing and harmless pranks.

Bolder feats brought fame to Anderl Heckmair, veteran alpinist and *Bergführer,* or mountain guide. A quiet-spoken man in his 60's, Anderl stands barely five feet tall and weighs less than 130 pounds. Yet among the fraternity of climbers, his name is legend. The reason is the giant called the Eiger.

I learned about the Eiger one evening over dinner with Anderl and Trudy in their home on the outskirts of Oberstdorf. Through friends in Munich I had an introduction to the Heckmairs, which Trudy quickly translated into an offer of a home-cooked meal. Over an Allgäu specialty — a delicious onion, cheese, and noodle dish called *Käsespätzle* ("cheese sparrows") — Anderl answered my questions about his climbing career.

Orphaned as a child, Anderl began work as a gardener's apprentice and later turned to the profession of bergführer. During the great era of mountain climbing in the 1930's he participated in a number of difficult climbs and finally challenged the Eiger in company with three other men.

The Eiger is a fearsome mass of rock standing 13,026 feet high in the Bernese Alps of central Switzerland. Until 1938, when Anderl's group challenged the peak, no one had ever succeeded in scaling its notorious north wall. It had already claimed the lives of half a dozen expert mountaineers, and many considered it unclimbable.

"We were lucky," Anderl said. "We encountered some difficult stretches, but we managed to work our way past them. The weather held, and we weren't delayed by storms. The climb took only three days, instead of the eight we had allowed for."

News of the event flashed across Germany. The country by then was in the grip of Nazism, with its cult of Aryan superiority. Germans everywhere hailed the conquest of the Eiger as a national triumph, and Anderl became a celebrity overnight.

Despite his triumph over the Eiger, Anderl's most memorable experience occurred in 1951, in the French Alpine region known as the Grandes Jorasses. With a single partner he set out to scale the vertical face of a 13,792-foot peak called the Walkerpfeiler.

Above 9,000 feet the two were caught in a snowstorm. With no hope of retreat they clung precariously to their ropes, swinging pendulum-like across the sheer face of the rock and waiting for the storm to subside.

It lasted six days and nights.

Finally, on the seventh day, the weather cleared and they inched their way to the top — only to be swept a thousand feet down the reverse slope of the mountain by an avalanche. Through some miracle they survived.

Luckily for me, many parts of the Allgäu Alps can be enjoyed without ice axes and crampons. One mist-shrouded morning I joined Anderl and Trudy on a cross-country ski trek over the Engenkopf, a 4,000-foot peak rising to the west of Oberstdorf.

With the mountaineer's disdain for cable cars and ski tows, Anderl chose a lovely wooded trail up the side of the mountain. Shouldering our skis, we hiked for an hour through dense stands of pine and spruce amid silence broken only by the occasional rustle of a mountain stream.

Above the 3,000-foot level the forest gave way to high Alpine meadow, heavily blanketed with snow and wrapped in a gauze of fine mist. Taking to our skis, we glided across a ghostly landscape dotted here and there by clusters of dwarf mountain birch and laced with the tracks of countless animals. Trudy identified each footprint on sight — *Gemse,* or chamois, fox, rabbit, deer, and the elusive *Schneehuhn,* or ptarmigan.

"Often Anderl and I encounter the animals themselves," she remarked. "They are quite fearless, for only a very few people come here any longer." She waved at the empty shell of a wooden *Heustadel,* or hay storage shed. "If farmers fail to cut or graze their own mountain pasture for three years in a row, the government makes them plant trees and turn the land back into forest."

Traversing a shoulder of the Engenkopf, we slalomed gently down the other side until the snow gave out and then hiked once more through the forest. Back in Oberstdorf we said goodbye and Anderl made me a generous offer.

"Come back again one day and we will go mountain climbing together." He winked. "Perhaps we will find another Eiger."

NOT LIKELY, although Castle Neuschwanstein in its way might be just as difficult for the beginner to climb — particularly if he were doing it through a medieval shower of boiling oil. No one has ever tried, for despite its awesome appearance, Neuschwanstein was built for pleasure, not defense. Unhappily, its owner barely lived to enjoy it.

Bavaria's most impressive castle stands some 25 miles northeast of Oberstdorf, on the scenic *Deutsche Alpenstrasse,* or German Alpine Road, that spans the entire Bavarian range, east and west. Towering above the Lech Valley on a natural pedestal of rock, Neuschwanstein displays a profusion of turrets, casements, and palisades that would bring tears to the eyes of a pastry chef. It also brought tears to the eyes of Ludwig II's financial advisers.

According to records in the Bavarian archives, this beloved but eccentric king spent

6,180,047 gold marks on its construction alone, to say nothing of furnishings. An assistant curator of the castle (now a public museum), kindly gave me a personal tour of its ornate chambers and a personal view of the cost. According to him, Ludwig spent his own gold, not Bavaria's.

"Historians often accuse the King of draining the royal treasury for his private benefit," he told me. "That is simply not true. Ludwig II was a Wittelsbach, the family that ruled Bavaria as an independent state from the 12th century well into the 19th. Ludwig was actually one of the last of the line, reigning from 1845 until his death in 1886, shortly after Neuschwanstein was completed.

"It is true that some of the Wittelsbachs were eccentric—one or two were actually insane—but they were scrupulously honest, and immensely wealthy. Whatever Ludwig did, he did out of his own pocket."

Bavaria by 1886 had ceased to be an independent state and had become, with Ludwig's reluctant but wise agreement, part of the German Empire. Yet his legacy to his people remains even now in the official title of their land: *Freistaat Bayern*—the Free State of Bavaria.

To the east of Neuschwanstein another legacy survives, a legacy of unquenchable faith in time of adversity. As it has for nearly three and a half centuries, the village of Oberammergau celebrates its historic deliverance from plague with a re-enactment every ten years of Christ's passion and death on the cross. The first play was presented in 1634; later ones were staged to coincide with the beginning of each decade.

Oberammergau's famous Passion Play is a deeply moving experience for the hundreds of thousands who attend it—more than half a million during the 1970 performances alone. For those who take part, the play is something of a collective miracle, uniting 4,600 villagers in a renewal of faith.

Oberammergau out of season—that is, roughly nine years out of ten—is an almost somnolent village, content in its traditional vocations of dairy farming and wood carving. Hospitality in the Alps, however, is hardly a once-in-a-decade custom and Mary Magdalene invited me to her home for coffee.

Her real name is Christl Fischer and she is 28, two years older now than when she played the role of the penitent harlot. I asked Frau Fischer how she was chosen for the part, and she shook her head. "It is a

Knapsack and rough-trimmed staff propped against a forest bench, an elderly Bavarian rests for a moment—listening, perhaps, for the rustle of a wary deer in the nearby thicket or the unmistakable call of a distant cuckoo.

matter of competition," she said, "and I do not really know. A committee of prominent villagers chooses the winners, and they do not generally explain their decision."

Requirements for the leading female roles are rigid; in addition to having a high degree of talent, every applicant must be single and under the age of 36. Frau Walter Fischer disqualified herself by marrying soon after the 1970 season. I asked if she would want her future children to take part in the play and she smiled.

"*Every* child of Oberammergau takes part," she answered. "All of them want to be in it, of course, and all are given a role in at least one mass scene." I had read that many Oberammergau families take pride in having supplied several generations of actors, and I asked Frau Fischer if her family was one.

"Yes," she answered politely. "My maiden name was Rutz, and one of our people helped to present the first Passion Play, in 1634. We have been involved in them ever since."

LONG BEFORE the Black Death ravaged Europe the White Death was taking its tearful toll in the Alps. "*Der Weisse Tod,*" as Germans call the avalanche, has claimed the lives and property of uncounted villagers down the ages. Not all the victims have been mountain people—the ten on the Zugspitze in 1965, for example, were visitors.

Along with hundreds of others they had picked that Saturday in late May to visit the country's highest mountain. After a pleasant morning's skiing, they had paused for lunch on the terrace of Schneefernerhaus, a hotel below the summit. The sun was warm, and like others on the terrace they dozed.

Somewhere on the peak above them a deadly equation was at work, an equation involving temperature, the slope incline, consistency and stratigraphy of snow. Slowly, inexorably, the factors combined to achieve a certain ratio exceeding the stability of the snow cover. The result was fatal.

"It was the first disaster of this kind we had," Oskar Reinwarth told me. A glaciologist, he had invited me on a visit by cable car to the summit of the Zugspitze, with a brief stop at Schneefernerhaus. On that day, long after the tragedy, the terrace was again jammed with guests and Herr Reinwarth swept a hand toward the crowd.

"That is about how it was when the avalanche struck," he continued. "Its speed was such that no one realized it was coming,

much less had time to escape. Nothing could save those directly in its path; 28 others were injured, but survived."

Probably the ten who died did so before the snow even touched them; with its enormous speed and mass, an avalanche builds up a violent wind ahead of it that can strike with deadly force.

I asked how it was that guests still used the terrace, and Dr. Reinwarth waved at a series of steel structures above us. "Those were put there after the accident, but they are only one line of defense.

"The primary one is a *Sprengbahn*—a steel cable running across the slope, equipped with explosive charges that can release the snow before it accumulates to the danger point." He shook his head grimly. "It is very effective, once some tragedy has shown the need for it."

This avalanche prompted protective measures at other critical points, and it formed a partial protection of snow cover on the glacier called Schneeferner—*Ferner* means "glacier" in dialect. This fact is important to Herr Reinwarth, for the Bavarian Alps have only four small glaciers left. To me the information seemed of interest only to glaciologists, but Herr Reinwarth explained that glaciers help to prevent alternate ravages of flood and drought in the lowlands.

"They work as vast storage tanks," he said, "accumulating snow during the winter and releasing meltwater in summer." He waved at the glistening expanse of the Schneeferner, and I understood that what happens there is of concern to all Germany.

What happens in the Zugspitze area is not only of concern but of considerable delight to most Germans. The region is far and away the most popular winter sport center of the Bavarian Alps, thanks to such villages as Garmisch-Partenkirchen and Mittenwald.

Garmisch-Partenkirchen handles more than 1.3 million overnight guests a year—with, to be sure, a certain inevitable confusion. On a busy midwinter weekend the streets are jammed with small glaciers of traffic and the sidewalks bristle with shouldered skis and poles like the muskets of some vast rabble army on the march.

At such times the Bavarian temper wears noticeably thin, and just as often finds its match in the pungent Bavarian sense of humor. The visitor whose schoolroom German is too urbane for arguments between irate motorists can test his own sense of humor in the souvenir shops that abound with grotesque memorabilia, such as *ersatz* chamois hoofs supporting a pink-shaded bedside table.

But when it comes to the business of mountain survival and rescue, Garmisch has few equals. An authority on racing introduced me to this aspect of Alpine life — Hanns Kilian, captain of the Olympic gold medal four-man bobsled team in 1934 and 1935, winner of a dozen other championships, coach and consultant to innumerable teams. Through him I met Hans Ettl and his German shepherd, Blanka. And through him I spent a morning with the *Bergwacht,* or "Mountain Watch," a Red Cross organization of some 4,000 crack skiers, stationed throughout the Alps on 24-hour call for rescue operations. With a 12-man team I lifted off in a German army helicopter for a simulated rescue in a remote area to the south. In 20 minutes after the chopper hovered over a clearing on a peak devoid of trails, the "victim" was being transferred to an ambulance.

As Hanns Kilian says, Garmisch is ready for almost anything.

Many of its smaller counterparts, happily, are neither ready nor willing to permit multistory hotels and other facilities out of keeping with Alpine character. (Television antennas escape the ban, and today many a roughhewn farmer's cottage boasts a profusion of wires and cables that would do credit to a military command post.)

Still, following the Deutsche Alpenstrasse once more, I passed a succession of small villages fitted like miniature cameos in the great pronged setting of the eastern Alps. Here increasing numbers of Germans come year round, avoiding the larger resorts in favor of such delightful retreats as Bayrischzell, Reit im Winkl, and Ramsau.

Meanwhile the younger generation of mountain people is moving the other way — to lowland cities, for education and jobs. A good many, however, return in later years to the villages where they were born. Certainly that is true of Berchtesgaden.

Eastern anchor of the Bavarian range and a historic lure in itself, Berchtesgaden attracted settlers as far back as the Bronze Age by virtue of a single powerful magnet — salt. Evidence suggests that early Europeans discovered and mined the rich deposits in the mountain known as Obersalzberg. Certainly, the Celts and the Romans gravitated to the area for the same reason, and Germans even today work the mines.

Salt, however, is but one of Berchtesgaden's assets, and a minor one at that. In addition to spectacular scenery and incomparable winter sports, the village offers an outstanding folk-opera company, a troupe specializing in the lively Bavarian dance known as the *Schuhplattler,* and craftsmen whose skill at fashioning wooden toys verges on magic. It is no accident that in the postwar era the U. S. Army agreed to relinquish nearly all its Alpine resort facilities except those at Garmisch and Berchtesgaden. But then, Hitler himself was reluctant to leave.

During World War II, Berchtesgaden won dubious fame as the mountain *Festung,* or bastion, of the Nazi hierarchy. At astronomical cost Germany's war leaders converted Obersalzberg into a combination resort and underground fortress. In the end it was abandoned with token resistance, for Hitler made his final stand in Berlin. All that remain are the empty bunkers and a building or two.

BERCHTESGADEN has at least one other subterranean retreat, according to local legend. Tradition maintains that the mountain known as Untersberg houses dwarfs who emerge at night to conduct pagan rites in Berchtesgaden's Christian churches.

Still another legend holds that Karl der Grosse, the Emperor Charlemagne, sleeps with his army in a cave beneath Untersberg. When the world's greatest injustice is committed, runs the tale, he and his comrades will sally forth to right it. Considering Hitler's crimes, one wonders just what sort of injustice the Emperor is waiting for.

A final myth persists despite patient denials—that stolen works of art valued in the millions were stored by the Nazis in Obersalzberg's salt mine during the war.

"We would have known about it, no matter how careful they were," Franz Lindmair told me the day I visited the mine. A senior engineer with the mining company, he had generously offered to show me about. As we made our way among a labyrinth of tunnels whose walls and ceilings glistened with millions of salt crystals, Herr Lindmair explained how the myth had arisen.

"Before the war," he said, "the Nazis did consider storing Germany's own works of art in the mine. They went so far as to try it, but the experiment failed—the salt air damaged the paintings. The only treasure in Obersalzberg is the salt itself."

Berchtesgadeners extract this treasure at a rate of some 160,000 tons of refined salt a year. The job cannot be hurried, for the salt is soaked out of the rock. Herr Lindmair showed me several of the giant chambers called *Sinkwerke* that are carved out of the crystalline rock, then flooded with water. Slowly the water filters down through the floor of the chamber, absorbing salt as it goes, and finally emerges in a storage basin below. From there, as a 27 percent solution, it is pumped out to huge distilleries.

"After ten years," Herr Lindmair said, "the layer of rock between the two chambers is dissolved away, and the space is only good for water storage. That is why we are constantly building new chambers—we have 14 in operation at the moment."

From time to time during our tour we encountered groups of helmeted miners and exchanged the traditional phrase, *"Glück auf!"* (Good luck!), always used underground in place of a more conventional greeting.

"Let us hope our luck continues," Herr Lindmair said. "We have not had a serious accident in more than seven years. Our people are among the very few miners in Germany who still pray together before they go underground."

There is, in fact, a certain cathedral atmosphere to Obersalzberg. For a finale Herr Lindmair took me deep in the mine to one of the brine basins. Descending a ladder through a vertical shaft, we emerged on a floating platform at the edge of a vast and darkened subterranean lake. In the light of our miner's lamps the stone ceiling winked and glittered with salt crystals like some immense canopy of sequined fabric.

Untying a makeshift raft, Herr Lindmair poled us around the giant grotto's 50,000 square feet of surface, past areas where the crystal ceiling swung low enough to graze our heads. It seemed a voyage to the very birthplace of the Alps, across the dark immensity of time and space to some legendary point of origin. In the deeper recesses of the grotto I half expected to glimpse the hurrying figures of dwarfs or the solitary bier of some long-ago warrior king.

At length Herr Lindmair turned back to the floating stage and before long we stood again at the entrance of the mine.

We shook hands then, and I thanked him. His reply was brief, but characteristic of his land and the people who inhabit the high Alps of Bavaria: *"Glück auf!"* □

THE NEAR-TROPICAL, dampish air was pungent with the scent of moist earth, flowers, and vegetation bursting with life. Castles, watchtowers, farm villages, and churches dotted the landscape, and the wide valley was bright with apple, pear, and peach orchards. Vineyards clung to the hillsides along the narrow road. There was a piquant whiff of insecticide—just to prove you were not quite in fairyland.

It was early May. I was nearing the old resort town of Merano in the Trentino-Alto Adige region, quite far east in the Italian Alps, near the Austrian border. Signs along the road—Burgstall, Brennerpass—were in German as well as Italian, for this was once Austrian South Tyrol, ceded to Italy in 1919.

German license plates and cars grew more numerous as I approached Merano. Later I learned that German visitors outnumber Italians by about four to one in this region.

I wanted to begin my trip in Merano because an old friend, Prince Boris degli Arodij de Rachewiltz, lives there in an honest-to-goodness castle with his wife, Mary, daughter of the poet Ezra Pound. On phoning Castle Brunnenburg I learned that Prince Boris, a well-known Egyptologist, had just returned from Morocco. Mary de Rachewiltz was at home too, busy with a translation of her father's works into Italian and a book of her own.

That night the three of us had dinner in Merano, and I remarked that apparently northerners—emperors, soldiers, poets, or tourists in Mercedes cars—always wanted to come south across the Alps. Prince Boris said: "This used to be a spa of the Habsburg monarchy and its horse-and-buggy jet set. Now, with the Brenner Pass open all year, the Germans and the Austrians find this a convenient way of going abroad without really leaving home. Although the Germans may have a bit of difficulty understanding the Tyrolean dialect, the local people have no problems understanding them.

"Generally," he added, "I think visitors are looking for the sun, the exotic vegetation—the palm trees. They enjoy our congenial soul and, naturally, our art and ancient monuments."

My thoughts (Continued on page 141)

Patient hands of Gardena Valley wood-carver Rudi Prinoth coax from chestnut a statue of St. Florian, the patron of Upper Austria.

6

Italy: Snow-fed Lakes, Majestic Valleys

By TOR EIGELAND
Photographs by the author

Faces and folk music reflect a persistent identity: South Tyrol belonged to the Austrian Empire until 1919, and years of political turbulence followed cession to Italy. Now Tyroleans concentrate on spirited affirmations of their past and on folk customs ranging from the otherworldly to the downright earthy. In the town of Tyrol, a Whitsuntide procession marches devoutly, with solemnity; neighboring musicians stolidly attack the local wurst. And in nearby Merano, Helga Platzer—costumed for Sunday or holiday—holds a silver-mounted drinking horn, proper vessel for wine or Schnaps.

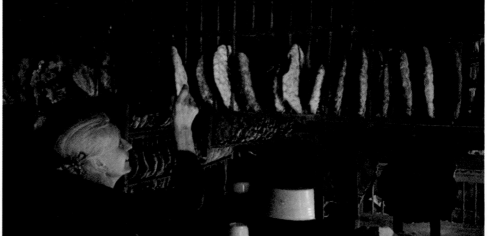

Mountain team: Peter Untermarsoner guides his family's prize-winning draft horse as it pulls a drag harrow on their farm near Ritten. Tyrolean bred, the blond-maned Haflingers are well adapted for high-country duty. This tableau of a man and a horse seems timeless, but Peter may be the last of his family to work these narrow fields. High-paying jobs have drawn away many young men and women who, like Peter, would prefer to remain in the mountains. Despite grueling labor, scant profit, and isolation, such Alpine farms keep a rewarding flavor of self-sufficiency. They provide their own milk, meat, vegetables, and bread—every spring, Frau Anne Untermarsoner bakes hundreds of wheat loaves, dries the bread, and stores it in attic racks for use all through the year.

Dozing on a bench at the center of Cortina, cattle-dealer Augusto Caldara indulges in a break from his genial role as a champion of the use of snuff. He offers it to everyone he meets. Here "Partel" — nicknames identify individuals in a town where surnames repeat themselves — pays quiet tribute to the excellence of lunch and perhaps to the quality of Dolomite wines. Dry white Sylvaner, the local favorite, comes of age in ancient casks under the attentive eye of Johann Sigmund in the 14th-century wine cellars at Novacella. Like their wines — like this woodcutter from Oberinn Ritten — mountain people often show traits of congenial aging. But in Italy no one overlooks the qualities of youth, in wines or in a lovely face; this girl works at her mother's newsstand in Stresa.

Beyond the Sexton Group of the Dolomites (foreground), the rounded peak of 10,705-foot Antelao breaks the misty far southern skyline near the famed resort town of Cortina.

GERHARD KLAMMET

Close race under the cliffs: in a regatta near Riva, sailors scud across the clean water of Lake Garda, largest of the Italian lakes. Clinging to the steep western shore, the Venetian-style buildings of Limone sul Garda reflect a beneficent sun. Travelers welcome Limone as a stop on the lakeside Riva-Gargnano road, which passes through 70 tunnels in only 18 miles. Like much else in the lake country, architecture often shows a mixture of styles; the cathedral at Como blends Gothic elements with Renaissance.

Working village since the Middle Ages, Isola dei Pescatori appears to float on the surface of Lake Maggiore. Its proud nickname, "the Republic," stems from its independent history as the only one of four islands in the Bay of Pallanzo not owned (and not extensively landscaped) by the powerful Borromeo family of Milano. In summer, jostling tourists crowd the cobbled streets. But fishing still sustains the island's life. Unloading their day's catch of lavarelli—whitefish—these men belong to a handful of families that have lived and fished here for centuries. In the evenings, with work done and tourists returned to the mainland, the new generation of islanders runs free. These youngsters "work" and romp outside a shop owned by their aunt, Signorina Carla Ruffoni.

Tending nets in winter fog, Lake Maggiore fishermen bend to their work under the walls of Castelli di Cannero—

once the lair of a murderous family of brigands whose cruelty was legendary, even by 15th-century standards.

High in the Valle d'Aosta at the hamlet of Graines, farmer Vincent Willermin (below) and his black-clad wife, Elena Borbey, watch their nephew Walter Revil, staff in hand, at his summer task of helping with the cattle. Two watering troughs and a dungheap flank the path. Animals occupy the ground floor, with family quarters above; the farthest door leads to a storeroom containing feed grains for the stock, cornmeal, potatoes, hard rye bread, and homemade sausage. Such stone farmhouses keep a long-established regional pattern. Architecture provides one of the few consistencies in an area where borders have shifted often, where villages only miles apart speak different languages.

Rare heavy snowfall immobilizes Vernante, some 30 miles from the Mediterranean. Energetic residents turn out to clear narrow streets and free their overburdened roofs.

At least one hard-shoveling citizen measures the odds for just keeping up with the rapidly falling snow, while others make the most of their chance for some slippery horseplay.

wandered briefly homeward to Norway. Its mountains are spectacular, but you do not find little outdoor cafés where you can sit and sip an espresso and philosophize.

Then I asked Prince Boris about the political rumblings and the bombings that used to take place here. He explained that the German-speaking Tyroleans had actively pursued their goal—some measure of self-government—until Italy and Austria reached an agreement on the question in 1948. "As you know, this province is presently autonomous under the Italian government."

One look at the menu had convinced me that "integration" was taking place. The first items were *Backerbsensuppe* and *Knödel-suppe*, Austrian soups with dumplings. The third and fourth: *Risotto* and *Pasta Asciutta*.

One day convinced me that Merano is a wonderful town for walking. Set in a sheltered valley, this little city has 40 miles of paths and promenades, shaded by cypress, cedar, magnolia, chestnut, pine, fig, and—yes—palm trees. In the "old town's" narrow Via dei Portici, every arcade has something to interest tourists or residents: boutiques, leather-goods stores, spotlessly neat butcher shops, fine little restaurants and *Weinstuben*.

A good hour's uphill walk brings you to the 12th-century Castle of Tyrol which gave its name to the nearby town of Tyrol as well as to the region. The castle, the town, and the people are all sturdy.

Most of the women wear wide skirts, mid-calf-length, in different colors, and blouses, usually white. Nearly all males wear the traditional vintner's blue apron and a little Tyrolean hat. It is evidently not necessary to make wine to wear the apron, only to drink it. Countless faces have acquired the fresh light-red glow of the excellent local wine.

The town is so Tyrolean it seems a bit unreal, invented for tourists. Yet, early one morning before most tourists had brushed their teeth, a solemn Whitsuntide procession wound its way through the streets. For all the gaily colored Tyrolean costumes, there were tears in many eyes and most of the marchers were praying in low tones as they walked along under wind-buffeted religious banners.

Impatient to see real Tyrolean countryside, I drove up the Passiria Valley one

Once a center of power, dating from the 12th century, Reifenstein Castle dominates only the flowers by the Brenner Pass autostrada.

morning toward the Giovo Pass. At first the valley was wide, heavily cultivated, with vineyards and apple orchards. Leaves in many tones of green sparkled after days of rain.

Just outside San Leonardo in Passiria, I stopped at a rambling farmhouse. In front, in the shade of big trees, two young girls were happily splashing each other across a watering trough. They greeted me—"*Grüss Gott!*"—and playfully sent a few drops of water in my direction, then resumed their game. A sign caught my attention—this was the birthplace of Andreas Hofer, "national hero" of the Tyrol. Hofer bravely led a successful insurrection against Bavaria in 1809 and has since acquired a status nearly divine. If a Tyrolean asks whether you visited this shrine, you should be able to say "yes."

ZIGZAGGING up the valley past Valtina, you leave the rich vineyards and orchards for a "milk and potato" culture. Pine and fir trees cover the hillsides. Scattered, hardscrabble mountain farms have a few cows, chickens, possibly some goats, a bit of pastureland and a few hayfields, a postage-stamp vegetable patch, and the odd cherry tree. Throughout the Italian Alps, across ethnic frontiers, I found this same kind of milk-and-potato economy at altitudes between approximately 2,000 and 5,000 feet.

As I drove up the valley, children were running down the road on their way to school. Though poor, they were warmly dressed—patches were neat, if numerous—with solid boots or shoes. They never tried to hitchhike, a common practice elsewhere in Italy.

Near the Passo di Monte Giovo, farms and trees vanished and patches of snow along the road grew bigger. The glorious, intense blues, whites, yellows of Alpine flowers covered everything that the snow had not taken care of. There were some stone huts that could be 50 or 500 years old—for cows on summer pasture.

With traffic barred except "at your own risk," I had seen neither man nor beast for some time. Snowbanks up to ten feet high were leaning dangerously into the road. Out of nowhere, a boy in a blue sweater, blue in the face from the cold, leaped into the road and shouted weakly, *"Eeeedelweiss!"* He held out a few flowers in his right hand. I was too surprised to stop. He surely knew that it is illegal to pick these rare flowers—and that some tourists buy them in summer.

Clouds had covered the pass itself. The

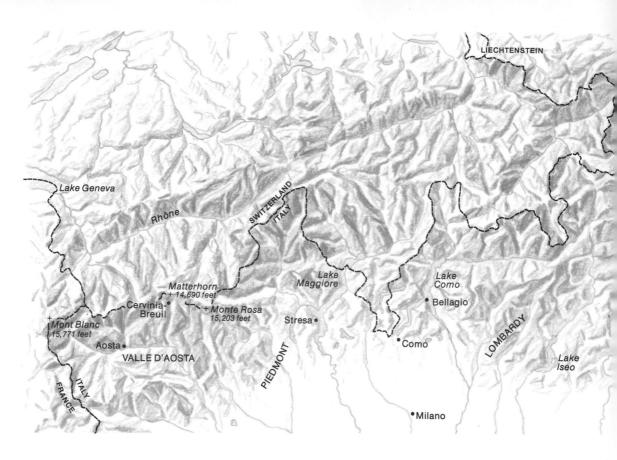

More persuasive than the many provincial and national borders, these mountains, valleys, and lakes define an area and its people. The result: a distinctly Alpine way of life, apparent even as early as the Bronze Age.

only sounds were the hushing of the wind and a staccato cuckoo call far in the valley.

Beyond, at Vipiteno, I joined the busy main thoroughfare from Germany and Austria. This route winds down from the Brenner Pass into the heartland of Italy.

Friends in Merano had advised me not to miss the wine cellar at the Augustinian convent of Novacella. The convent, never closed since the 12th century, turned out to be a number of buildings varying in style from a circular, fortified 12th-century chapel through Romanesque to a baroque church and 20th-century living quarters.

Deep in the cavelike wine cellar, the *Kellermeister,* Herr Franz Markart, said: "In 1300 they made the wine cellar, and next the cloister so they would always have wine." He used pidgin German to make sure I understood: "Casks all wood. Oakwood. Many casks 200 years old, two inches thick. No

Brenner Pass
Vipiteno
Isarco
AUSTRIA
ITALY
San Leonardo
in Passiria •
Tyrol •
• Merano
Bressanone
Adige
• Ortisei
Ritten •
Bolzano •
TRENTINO-ALTO ADIGE
• Cortina
d'Ampezzo
Marmolada +
10,965 feet
Adige
VENETO
Riva •
• Torbole
• Limone
• Malcesine
Gargnano
Lake
Garda
Vonico •
• Verona

leaks. Wine always good. Here white wine — 70 percent white wine. Here red — 30 percent. Most popular is Sylvaner. Dry white."

Upstairs a snack bar earns revenue for the convent, charging very reasonable prices. Hired waiters in blue aprons serve fresh local bread, cheese, and *Speck*. Speck, a smoked bacon often cured in chimneys, is one of the great delicacies of the Tyrol.

Just down the road, at the ancient town of Bressanone, you find another regional delight. Bressanone is famous for two things: the Hotel Elefante, named after an elephant that passed through in 1515 on its way from the court of Suleiman the Magnificent to the court of the Archduke Maximilian, and the Elephant Plate. The latter, naturally, is served at the Hotel Elefante.

The manager of the hotel, Wolfgang Heiss, Jr., had that day received his first issue of NATIONAL GEOGRAPHIC — a gift. He was so pleased he offered me an *Elefantenplatte* right on the spot. Since the dish is normally prepared for at least four people, I told him I would prefer just to see one.

Herr Heiss took me into the restaurant just as a steaming mound of food was brought to a happy table. One great platter held braised,

boiled, smoked, roasted beef, tongue, ribs, veal, and sausages, all surrounded by luscious fresh vegetables. The guests invited me to sit down and participate in the defeat of this dish, which I happily did.

Fräulein Dr. Elfi Prinnegg, an attractive young veterinarian from Merano, joined me next day to visit a farm near Ritten — and from Ritten, looking east across the Isarco Valley, I had my first magnificent view of the Dolomites, half shrouded in storm clouds.

Alois and Anne Untermarsoner and their grown son, Peter, were seated around a large wooden table when we dropped in. They promptly asked us to join them in a delicious lunch of knödelsuppe, hard wheat bread, speck, and wine. As we waited for coffee, I found that a conspicuous snoring I had heard was emanating from a large St. Bernard dog sprawled under the table on the well-scrubbed wooden floor.

Comfortable details marked their big dining-living room: aging family photos around the yellow-painted walls, a big cabinet-model late-'20's radio, calendars from local shops, a picture of the Virgin, a statue of Christ between the Virgin and St. Joseph. The rear section of the kitchen oven protruded into the room, to serve as a heater and clothes drier in winter. A grandfather clock ticked away in a corner.

I asked Alois, a fine fiftyish farmer type with a big moustache and crinkly warm eyes, how old his farm was. *"Ach,"* he said, "it must be 'round about three or four hundred years old now." Had they done any renovations to the house? "No, we haven't done anything like that except for a bit of paintin' recently." Then he added, looking unmistakably pleased, some significant recent news: "Our Haflinger horse won first prize in three-year-olds the other day."

Of course we had to go out and have a look at the horse. The stocky straw-colored Haflinger immediately nuzzled both Peter and Alois, and seemed just as pleased as the rest. In the stable I noticed six cows and two calves. Alois told me that they also kept pigs, a couple of dozen hens, some cats, and bees. They sold some of the pigs, speck, and butter, Anne mentioned.

Both the barn and the house were typical of that vicinity, with steep, gabled, red-tiled roofs. The attic of the house was used to store personal things, mostly, but also racks and racks of bread. Anne told me that they made about 600 loaves once a year, in spring, then let it dry for storage. And she proudly showed us a little house which was really a huge stone-lined oven.

Peter, a tall, husky man, shyly opened his mouth for the first time, explaining that they had some apple, pear, cherry, and walnut trees. "And a corn and 'tato patch."

Elfi asked whether Peter was engaged yet. Peter looked away and it was his mother who spoke up: "Oh—that is a little difficult. Difficult, it is." She sighed. Elfi told me later that this is a very serious matter on all the little uneconomical mountain farms—young people who want to stay at home cannot find partners.

Back in Merano, Elfi and I discussed the future of such farms, and of the region. Did she think the Tyrol would remain German-speaking? "For the next hundred years, yes." Thoughtfully, she added: "After that the question will not any more be really important because we will have a Europe where nationality won't make as much difference."

She went on to say things that I heard and saw elsewhere as well: "People now travel. Labor moves around. All these small places will disappear. All these typical things will be just for tourists. The Tyrolean farm way of life will disappear. Life is too hard for them. They have no money and they work hard. The only way many of them can survive is by renting out rooms." She obviously felt this strongly; it simply rushed out of her, regret in her normally cheerful voice.

Elfi Prinnegg is an internationalist first, as well as a good Italian and a patriotic Tyrolean. I kept her attitude in mind as I drove from Merano to Cortina d'Ampezzo in the heart of the eastern Dolomites. Cultural borders are so marked that to travel across the Italian Alps is almost like experiencing several different countries.

In Roman times there was a strong central rule, a security which vanished in the Middle Ages when each castle came to be the "capital" of a small domain. Beyond each little state all kinds of dangers lurked. Castles are no longer centers of power, but regionalism is still strong.

Increasingly, however, Italians are becoming very mobile. The comforting hiss of espresso machines, Fiats, and signs in Italian now dispel any doubt as to where you are.

Cortina is roughly 50 miles east of Merano as the jet flies. By car on a good road it takes three to four hours, and you encounter three completely different languages. Italian is pretty well understood everywhere. Tyrolean German is spoken in most of the Trentino-Alto Adige. Beyond Bolzano you enter the Veneto region, and here, around the Sella Group of the Dolomites, people speak Ladin. A Romance language, incomprehensible to outsiders, it is said to be the closest thing to live, colloquial Latin.

Rain cascaded down nearly the whole way to Cortina, and so did a few rocks from the slopes. About 20 miles southwest of Bolzano I stopped to see if tiny Lake Carezza would be visible. Just as I walked out to a clearing in the pines, the clouds broke and the sun burst down on this crystal-clear green lake and, behind it at close quarters, the Latemar Range of the Dolomites.

IN THE ALPS I saw taller peaks and bigger mountains, but this little lake has remained engraved in my mind. Inadvertently I had left my tape recorder running and when I replayed a tape that night I heard a big "wow!" from Lake Carezza.

Farmhouses around Cortina looked slightly different from those of South Tyrol. They employed more wood, and many houses had a balcony all around the top floor, protected by overhanging, slanted roofs.

In some of these mountain villages, the peasants may paint a window onto a blank wall. They paint curtains for it, flower pots, and even a person looking out. I never ascertained the origin of this custom, but it is a mere sample of how you could spend years exploring a single Alpine valley without becoming bored.

Cortina itself, strung along the junction of the Bigontina and Ampezzo Valleys amid superb peaks, has few old buildings left. And when I called on businessman Rinaldo Zardini, an expert on the Dolomites, he and his attractive wife greeted me in a cleanly elegant contemporary apartment with a living room dominated by something that looked like a sculpture by Henry Moore.

In fact this object, about two and a half feet tall, belonged to Signor Zardini's collection of fossils, most of them stored in an alcove just off the living room. As he explained: "This big bivalve is really the inside part of a giant shell, about 200 million years old, when the temperature here was tropical. What you see is a natural cast, the exact shape in rock. Others are real shells, but they are only found in very high rock formations—much younger formations."

Obligingly, he went on to tell me more about the Dolomites: "They got their name from the French geologist Déodat Gratet de Dolomieu, who spent a good part of his life back in the 18th century studying these rocks. Chemically they are a carbonate of calcium and magnesium. More dramatically put, they are altered coral reefs that were buried and then pushed out of the sea by mountain-building forces deep in the earth."

"And what about farming here?"

Replied Signor Zardini: "It doesn't amount to much any more. People cannot compete with mechanized farming farther south. They still keep a few cows and some chickens, but you need a few hundred cows to make money.

"No, this is becoming a hundred percent tourist economy. Let me tell you—in 1860 there were two or three simple hotels here. By 1900 there were 15 hotels. Now there are over 80. People live well and easily here now. It is beautiful—and there is no pollution."

For beauty, everyone in Cortina told me, the famous "Tour of the Five Passes" is a must. This route surrounds the Sella Group, with passes at about 7,000 feet above sea level. Funiculars and lifts offer dizzying rides to perennially snow-clad peaks.

I set off at six o'clock one sunny morning, and when I returned that evening about seven I was astonished to see that my odometer had clocked off only a hundred miles—the hairpin curves and sharp turns must have run into thousands. Some of the sharpest are cobbled for better traction, with a speed limit of 7 kilometers (4.4 miles) per hour. The tour resembles a whole day on the world's grandest roller-coaster, among spiraling mountain peaks and deep green valleys.

The first pass, Falzárego, was the scene of bloody battles during World War I. As I reached the crest, the mighty Marmolada, highest of the Dolomites at 10,965 feet, shimmered in the distance. The enormous silence made machine guns and bloodshed seem incongruous to the point of absurdity.

An hour later, at the Pordoi Pass, I stopped to watch some young Italians at a mountain-climbing lesson. A girl slipped, dropped, let out a piercing scream. The instructor cheerfully shouted, "Did she fall? A bottle of wine!" He knew, of course, that she was safe on a strong rope.

Approaching the Sella Pass I felt that a few thousand feet of mountains were leaning over me. A sign said: "Danger of Avalanche."

Several cars had stopped; so did I, expecting an accident. Everyone was staring up at the Piz Ciavazes. It took me about five minutes to spot two specks—two people climbing. One was inching his way out and up, with nothing but air beneath him, to get around an overhanging bit of rock. I imagined the view these brave souls had—looking 2,000 feet straight down—and found my own unnerving enough. Even on the road, even at a pass, you rapidly gain a lot of respect for these mountains.

Before leaving the Dolomites for Lake Garda and points west, I wanted to see the famous wood carving of the Ladin-speaking Gardena Valley. When I drove into Ortisei, "capital" of the Gardena wood-carvers, children were strolling back to school after lunch, chatting in Ladin. I asked them in Italian where I could find a good wood-carver. This set off an animated discussion. The consensus was reported politely in good Italian: "Go and see Mr. Rudi Prinoth. He works just down the street on the right-hand side."

I don't know whether young Rudi Prinoth was the best wood-carver in Ortisei, but he was certainly good. Olive-skinned and black-haired, with sharp Latin features, he looked very different from his Tyrolean neighbors.

His store also served as a workshop, crammed with sculpture to the rafters. I asked if he would continue working while I took photographs and asked questions. "Of course," he nodded.

"Carving is an old tradition here," he told me. "It started about three hundred years ago. Our valley was full of farmers. In the winter they had nothing to do, so they started carving wood. Now we study for six years in our School of Wood Carving and Design before we really get going. Much now is machine work, but there are still many of us who carry on with the real thing."

"What kind of wood do you use?"

"Pine and chestnut, mostly pine. Most of our sales are to Germany, Austria, and Switzerland. Also to Italy—religious articles mainly, saints for churches—but the others are closer. Now some American dealers also come through and buy quite a lot."

I asked if the use of Ladin presented a problem in a largely German-speaking area where the official language is Italian. He replied: "Only a few old-timers speak Ladin exclusively. We all learn German and Italian in school, and some also speak English."

A party of Austrian tourists entered and

excitedly started to look around. Signor Prinoth winked. It was time to go.

At Bolzano I entered the Milano *autostrada,* which lets you barrel through the Adige Valley in no time at all. It seemed disrespectful to this majestic valley, inhabited since Neolithic times, to sprint along without a speed limit. But it was exhilarating after weeks of negotiating hairpin turns.

Then, spread out before me from a hilltop lookout point, was the northern end of turquoise Garda, biggest of the Italian lakes. On my side of the lake, the eastern, olive, citrus, and cypress trees gave the scene a distinctly Mediterranean look.

I drove down to Torbole, a charming little port with Venetian aspects, like most of the Garda towns. However, Riva, only a mile and a half to the north, is definitely Austrian-Tyrolean in its architecture; it was an Austrian lake port until it was surrendered to Italy in 1919.

At Riva I had the good fortune of checking into the Hotel du Lac et du Parc. The concierge immediately loaded me down with booklets and pamphlets and said, "You have to try our red Bardolino wine for dinner." Then he told me of foods I had to sample, and places to go. His judgment was sound.

On his advice, next morning, I drove south along the western shore on the excellent "Gardesana" road that encircles the lake. The Gardesana clings to the mountainside — or goes through it by way of tunnels and galleries, some only 30 or 40 feet apart. Tall, elegant cypresses shot into view between each tunnel.

EIGHT MILES' DRIVE finds a little gem of a town — Limone sul Garda — strung along the shore. Limone is a town of pergolas, rosebushes, lemon trees, cobblestone streets and stone steps. Its tiny lanes wind themselves through little tunnels, up through hillsides, under fig trees, past quaint little harbors with fishing boats, rowboats, and pleasure craft for hire. There are old churches built of stone, small hotels and restaurants with vine-covered terraces conducive to sitting for hours — which I did. One little lane I saw had 31 steps, each with two potted geraniums. Grapevines covered every bit of space not otherwise occupied.

Supposedly Limone had the first lemon grove in Europe and thus acquired its name. Now, according to a fruit vendor in the market, "we only grow a few lemons for fun. We find it much easier and more profitable to sell ice cream to the German and Danish tourists who come here."

Later that day I drove around to Malcesine on the eastern shore to visit Mr. John Bushell, English owner of the comfortable little Hotel Riviera. Over tea by the shore, I commented that Lake Garda looked remarkably clean. "The lake is totally unpolluted," he said. "There is no factory of any sort contaminating it, nor does any raw sewage flow into it. Fortunately, people here have seen what has happened to other lakes and they have taken precautions. Since ours is a tourist economy this is essential."

Lake Garda enjoys a mild climate, as the olive and citrus trees indicate. Snow may fall a hundred feet above lake level, but rarely along the shore. Great glaciers from the Central Alps gouged out deep lake beds from Garda to Maggiore, and these huge masses of water retain heat enough to moderate the climate through the winter.

Before leaving for Lake Maggiore I made a short sentimental side trip almost due west to the pass of Pian delle Fugazze in the shadow of massive Monte Pasubio. As a fan of Ernest Hemingway's, I wanted to see where he spent three weeks driving an ambulance in the spring of 1918.

At the pass I stopped; a gray haired, dignified gentleman and his wife came over, said "good day," introduced themselves — they were from Bolzano — and offered me some lemon cookies. Obviously he wanted to say something, and finally he came out with it: "You know, there were some terrible battles here in The War." For the first time I heard a World War I veteran talk about his combat experience.

He made clear why it was *The* War: he had fought here for more than a year. "He was wounded twice," added his wife.

"Did you know," he asked, "that your writer Hemingway drove an ambulance here?" I told him yes, and asked if he had met Hemingway. The old man told me he had seen some young Americans, but did not know their names.

After this conversation I lost the desire to visualize Hemingway in these hills. Hemingway had really come for a lark. He got his severe wound later, northeast of Venice.

The Serenissima, an excellent road with nothing serene about it, sped me west toward Como the next morning. Bypassing Milano, I zoomed along in smog. Prosperity and nature are at odds here. Industry in the south uses waterpower from the Alps — sending smog and cars back.

In the heavy traffic and haze, Como reminded me of a Milano suburb at first, but at Piazza Cavour on the waterfront my gloom was dispelled. Piazza Cavour is lined with hotels, shops, and sidewalk cafés full of Italians sipping espresso; it looks out on a cheerful variety of craft from hydrofoils to steamers and rowboats, the blue lake itself gleaming beyond.

Como, like most of northern Italy, has had a confusing, turbulent history. Etruscans and Celts were here before the Romans. After the Roman Empire faded, Como was conquered and reconquered and kicked around by — most recently — the French, the Spanish, and the Austrians, until Garibaldi liberated it from the latter in May 1859. Local dialect reflects all of the above influences.

On my first evening in Como I dined at an outdoor restaurant across the piazza from the Cathedral of Santa Maria Assunta, which one authority calls "perhaps the most perfect building in Italy for illustrating the fusion of Gothic and Renaissance styles." All traffic is banned from the square. I sat in peace and admired the unobtrusively lighted duomo; here, for some mysterious reason, the pigeons at night shriek in an eerie, strangely musical manner that I have never heard anywhere else.

More than the city of Como, it was probably the lake itself, the lush vegetation, the green hills and snow-clad mountains that inspired a "who's who" of great names. Pliny the Elder and Pliny the Younger were born here; Franz Liszt came visiting, as did Bellini and Rossini, Napoleon, and scandal-haunted Princess Caroline of Wales.

Shelley, house-hunting at Como, wrote: "The union of culture and the untameable profusion and loveliness of nature is here so close, that the line where they are divided can hardly be discovered." When Winston Churchill came here in September 1945 to rest after the latest liberation, he said he had never in his life painted as well.

Como's Provincial Tourist Board treats everyone like royalty. There I met Signor Ferruccio Brenna, a thirtyish, enthusiastic soul who cheerfully explained the ways of life around the lake.

One day we walked through the dreamlike gardens of Villa Carlotta, built in 1747, through a park ablaze with magnolias, azaleas, and jasmine. Like many others, this villa now belongs to the Italian state, and I remarked that the big private villa seemed to be a thing of the past.

"Some of the rich people from Milano still own villas here," said Signor Brenna, "but they rarely come. The trend is now toward the seashore, travel abroad, staying in hotels. People cannot afford the staff for a villa like this. At Villa Carlotta one would need at least 20 gardeners alone!"

Still, every bit of spare hilly land shows the effort of industrious farmers who grow olives, grapes, fruit, vegetables, and some wheat. Signor Brenna confided that some of the most industrious also do a bit of smuggling, bringing cigarettes across the mountains from Switzerland, a short hike away.

Industry, as I learned from Dottore Emilio Canibus at the Provincial Tourist Board, leaves tourism running about number four. "Silk and textiles have traditionally been our main industries," he said. "Our secret lies in superb design. Then we have hundreds of furniture factories in the region. There are also foundry products, and some lighter manufacturing like X-ray equipment and motorcycles." Fortunately, I thought, all this has not yet seriously blemished "the union of culture and the untameable profusion and loveliness of nature" at Lake Como.

UNLIKE the other great Italian lakes, Lake Maggiore is not entirely in Lombardy. Its western shore lies in Piedmont, and the northern end stretches into Switzerland. Historically, though, Maggiore has been bound up with Lombardy. And the Borromeo family, who even today own some of the islands as well as the fishing rights, have dominated the lake since the 15th century.

Lake Maggiore has special memories for me. I was there for ten days early in March, under a steady downpour. The standard greeting was *"Che brutto tempo! Sessanta giorni!* — What brutal weather! Sixty days!" Rain had indeed fallen for sixty days straight. A five a.m. to five p.m. fishing trip was probably the wettest, coldest experience of my life. (But we did catch a lot of fish.)

In many ways Lake Maggiore resembles Lake Como: the same rich vegetation, the great villas with their formal gardens, the spectacular setting, the old towns that range from sophisticated resorts like Stresa to unassuming fishing villages.

To me, Lake Maggiore means something more personal and more specific — Isola dei

Pescatori (Fishermen's Island) and the people I met there. It lies a long stone's throw from Stresa. Alexandre Dumas once defined it as "a charming joke which resembles a small village.... The nets, which form the riches of its two hundred inhabitants, are suspended before each door."

Pescatori is not a joke, but it is charming. The inhabitants now number 120, with, to quote a friend, "80 cats—no mice." A few little hotels and souvenir stands operate in summer only. The stands are especially ungreedy. At one I spotted a book about the island, in English, and asked the price. The island woman at the counter replied: "Don't buy it. The books are too expensive. Return it when you've finished it."

Not a soul was in sight when I arrived in March, in driving rain, but I found a café. I asked for a *cappuccino* and for Signor Angelo Cattalani, reputed to speak English and therefore in charge of foreign affairs. He turned out to be a 24-year-old student, a part-time fisherman, an artist, a good friend. Once I asked how he found time to study, since he had to commute to his university in Milano for civil-engineering courses. He said cheerfully: "It's difficult. When I'm tired I don't study and when I'm not tired I don't study because I'm not tired!"

Angelo took me for a walk to show me the island. In a hurry, you can walk the length of it in five minutes and across it in one minute. But we were not in a hurry. Pescatori is a medieval village, almost intact, and we saw it all. We walked cobblestone streets between rustic houses and through tunneled arches. We climbed outside stairways for a better look at things, and struggled along some little rocky beaches.

"In the Middle Ages," Angelo told me, "there were about 500 people here and 22 or 23 fishing boats. Most of the families here date back to that time. You'll find that nearly everyone is called Ruffoni, Zacchera, or Gottardi." Why had the population dwindled to 120? "Some years ago there were even fewer. People went away because the fishing was bad. In the last five years or so, many have come back because fishing has improved or to work in the tourist business."

Touring a fishermen's island means seeing the harbor. The basin was protected by a statue of the Madonna as well as a solid stone wall. Five diesel-engined boats rested on a sloping landing. Angelo explained: "There are ten boats now, two men to each.

Safe harbor, Lake Maggiore: between fishing and studying, the author's friend Angelo Cattalani naps at the feet of the Madonna on the stone breakwater of Isola dei Pescatori.

Not all of them went out today because of the wind. There are also four or five like me, who fish semiprofessionally. There are 22 kinds of fish in the lake, but what we sell are *alborelle, lavarelli,* perch, and some lake trout."

Under June sun, with plane trees in leaf and flowers in bloom, the island looked very different. People were strolling up and down the waterfront. Women were sitting on doorsteps chatting, or arranging their souvenir stalls. Children played in the streets, and all the cats were out promenading. Sidewalk cafés had opened. During the day boatloads of tourists came, strolled around, had a drink or a meal, and left. At night a warm, family sort of quiet took over, undisturbed by cars or motorcycles.

Angelo made a point of telling me, one day: "You know, this is *not* a Borromeo island. People still call this island 'the Republic.' It used to be a free port when the Stresa side belonged to the Kingdom of Piedmont and the Lombardy side was Austrian. You see that island over there?" He pointed to Isola Bella about 300 yards away. "That's a Borromeo island. We call it 'the Golden Rock.'"

On Isola Bella, wall-to-wall souvenir stands and restaurants crowd outside the gardens of Palazzo Borromeo, but you feel that no one really lives there. I wished I could have seen the island in the 17th century, when the Borromeos built their palace.

In the Valle d'Aosta, westernmost and last of the Alpine regions I visited, the speedy autostrada offers hints of earlier centuries. Almost as if from a low-flying plane, I saw old villages and towns snuggled comfortably along the bottom of the valley or clinging to the hillsides. Grapevines seemed to grow wherever man could conceivably scramble his way. In places the valley narrowed to a slit, easily defensible. Here, invariably, stood a fortress or a castle.

Today the Autonomous Region of the Valle d'Aosta, like the Trentino-Alto Adige, is self-governing within the Italian Republic. It peacefully shares its two Alpine giants, Mont Blanc and the Matterhorn, with France and Switzerland respectively. Tunnels supplement the famous passes used in Roman times, the Great St. Bernard linking Aosta with Switzerland, the Little St. Bernard leading into France.

Roman remains caught my eye on my first morning in Aosta, the regional capital. Just outside of town the indestructible stones of a Roman bridge now span a dried-up channel. I found this bridge especially attractive because it is still in use after 2,000 years. Motorcycles, cars, pedestrians, and a parade of dogs crossed over while I was watching. To them it was just something they crossed over. One of the dogs in particular showed no reverence at all.

I passed the Arch of Augustus (commemorating the defeat of the Salassi), parked my car, and walked under the Porta Praetoria, a double gateway of three arches set into fortified walls. Beyond the Roman theater I reached an office to keep an appointment with Beppe Brunier, a man as *simpatico,* happy, and easygoing as his name sounds.

Not only was Beppe born in the valley, he was born in the castle of Fenis, where his parents were caretakers—"I fought many a brave battle in that castle when I was a boy." Widely traveled, he speaks English, French, and the regional patois as well as Italian, and he gave me a spirited briefing as we drove toward the Gressoney Valley.

"Since the Paleolithic period the Alps have been inhabited. Neanderthal man used to hunt cave bears here. Much later the celticized Salassi lived in the Valle d'Aosta. Because they controlled the Great St. Bernard Pass as well as silver and gold mines, the Romans conquered them in 25 B.C."

In a rather intangible way, the people here seemed quite different from those of other regions I had visited. I mentioned this, and Beppe nodded: "We have our own kind of people all around the mountain [Mont Blanc]. We are just the same, all mixed up from Burgundians, Celts, Romans, and French-Burgundians. The dialect is an old French one, although the French don't understand us. This used to be part of the Duchy of Savoy."

As we entered the town of Issime, in the Gressoney Valley, the architecture seemed out of place. "Beppe, this reminds me of the Tyrol," I said. He laughed, pointing to a sign that read *"Municipio Mairie Gemeindehaus"* —"Town Hall" in Italian, French, and German.

"The settlers here," he said, "probably came from the Swiss Valais around the 14th or 15th century. They spoke a German dialect and still do. The next town, Gaby, is French-speaking—only a couple of miles away. A few miles farther up from Gaby, they speak a German dialect again."

How, I wanted to know, do the people of the valley get along? Beppe said, a little cautiously: "Relations are correct—I doubt that a visitor would ever notice friction."

Having noticed a layer of smog in some places at the bottom of the valley, I asked about manufacturing in Valle d'Aosta. "Yes," said Beppe, "it is not yet a big thing here, but there is a steel factory in Aosta, they make artificial silk in Chatillon, and in Verrès there is an aluminum plant."

Now, high in the Gressoney Valley, the sky was clear—and tokens of change were clear also. Here as elsewhere in Aosta, nearly all the old houses are built entirely of stone. A traditional house uses the ground floor as a stable. Above, benefiting from the animal heat, are living quarters; then the attic. Topping the stone tile roof—a TV antenna!

NEXT DAY, at Cervinia-Breuil, farming and husbandry had disappeared altogether; this may well be the most popular ski resort in Italy. Beyond multistory super-modern hotels, you look straight up at the stark Matterhorn. To its right is Monte Rosa.

On a warm, sunny June morning we took the cable car up to Plateau Rosa on the Swiss border, where at 11,480 feet it was still warm and sunny. Ears popping, we stepped into heavy snow and a big crowd of holiday-makers. Some wore ski clothes, others walked around in shorts or even bikinis.

Here ski lifts branch off in all directions, and a helicopter service will deposit the really jaded skier on any desired peak. Skiers also have the choice of taking themselves back into Italy or down to Zermatt, in Switzerland. I settled for a couple of glorious runs toward Cervinia-Breuil—attempting a yodel on the way.

That glamorous world seemed centuries removed the following morning. Beppe and I were near the little hamlet of Vetan, well above tree level at about 7,000 feet. Short, sinewy Umberto Pallé, his young assistants Giuseppe and Piero Jocallaz, and his diligent sheep dog Lola were tending some hundred cows and a few sheep.

Umberto kept growling *"aaaaaaach"* to direct willing little Lola while Giuseppe, a boy of about ten, was telling me some of the cows' names: "Campanella, Fragola, Violetta, Bellina, Bianca...."

Perhaps it was because I was leaving the next day that the purity of this scene touched me—the sunny fragrance of the meadow, the great mountains, and the brassy clanking of the cowbells which we could still hear plainly after herd and herdsmen were out of sight. □

RUSSET STREAKS of dawning sunlight banded an amethyst sky, visible only in patches above the dense forest I hiked through. Bells clanged discordantly and a tufted tail sporadically whisked past my face, slapping the stocky beast sauntering before me.

As the sky slowly lightened, the indistinct shapes of a dozen brown-and-white Pinzgauer milch cows took sharper form. Nearby strode dairy farmer Franc Cvetek, occasionally shouting a crisp command to a wandering cow. Earlier that June morning I had joined 67-year-old Franc on the yearly movement of cattle to summer pasture high in the Julian Alps of Slovenia, the northernmost republic of the Socialist Federal Republic of Yugoslavia.

The Alps tumble into Gorenjska—highland Slovenia—from Italy and Austria, forming three ranges. The Julians, the predominant group, are bold, rocky giants crowned by 9,393-foot Triglav. The Karavanke are jutting green-clad mountains on the Austrian border, and the Kamniške Alpe, the easternmost range, descend into rolling hills as the Alps taper to an end. Dividing these ranges are three rivers—the Soča and two branches of the Sava.

"We must start long before dawn," Franc had told me the day before, "because the cows won't climb if the sun gets too hot." Stars still spiked the sky when I met him at 3 a.m. on the trail to Grintovca, the mountain we were bound for. An hour later we were under way, following a dancing creek.

Several herds of 5 to 15 cattle, a few hundred feet apart, were climbing to the high meadows that morning. "Each herd belongs to a different family from Studor, my village, or Stara Fužina," Franc explained.

He walked with a gait as steady and sure as his cattle, a solid man accustomed to a life of work. A thin graying moustache, lively brown eyes, and a quick grin highlighted his face and a green felt hat topped his close-cropped hair. "The grasses in the *planine*—the high plateaus—are lush now, good for producing rich milk to make Bohinj cheese. The cows and some herders will stay there making cheese until the end of September."

The trail abruptly veered from the stream and began the *(Continued on page 165)*

7

Slovenia: Winter Hearth to Summer Trails

By WILLIAM R. GRAY
Photographs by JAMES P. BLAIR

Winter's work: On a chill February morning, farmer Franc Cvetek mends a handmade hay rake under the wide eaves of his house.

Tugging at a halter, Franc Cvetek leads his draft ox from a kozolec—a large shed for drying and storing hay—near the village of Studor. In the kitchen of their two-century-old home, three generations of the Cvetek family gather for Sunday dinner. Like his father, Franc relies on dairy farming for a livelihood; but the expansion of tourism brings additional income—the Cveteks own a new guesthouse. At a tavern on Saturday afternoon, Franc enjoys a drink and a chat with neighbors. His daughter Ivanka holds Marjana, the youngest of five grandchildren.

Stark figures etched against fog and snow, church-bound faithful (above) plod slowly from Studor to Srednja Vas, a neighboring village, on a drizzly Sunday morning. Work-roughened hands fold in prayer during the Roman Catholic Mass said in Slovene, a Slavic tongue. After the service, parishioners file homeward from the 400-year-old church.

Shadows of a June afternoon lengthen in a field by Lake Bohinj as Franc Cvetek and his family rake and pitch fresh-mown hay onto a cart. Franc's wife, Špela, takes a moment's pause; ten-year-old Milan, the eldest grandchild, pole-vaults with a grablje, a hay rake. In the summer, Franc moves his dozen milch cows from valley fields to mountain meadows; winter snows confine the animals to a barn in Studor where they live on hay.

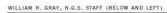

3 DIANTHUS MONSPESSULANUS L.

6 PHYTEUMA ORBICULARE L.

4 LILIUM CARNIOLICUM BERNH.

1 SILENE VULGARIS (MOENCH) GARCKE

2 CALTHA PALUSTRIS L.

5 LEONTOPODIUM ALPINUM CASS.

North wall of Triglav—Yugoslavia's highest peak, at 9,393 feet—plunges more than a mile to the Vrata Valley, bright with vivid wildflowers. Though photographed in the meadows and mountains of Slovenia, the varieties shown here extend their range through the Alpine region. To many the symbol of the Alps' beauty—and a famous souvenir—edelweiss (5) grows at high altitudes, thriving under legal protection. Radiant petals of the golden apple (4), another protected species, curl skyward; this lily belongs to the eastern Alps. Dainty hooks tip slender petals of the round-headed rampion (6). The fringed pink (3) and spiderlike bladder campion (1) flourish in fields and pastures. Poisonous to livestock, marsh marigolds (2) blossom in bogs or damp woods.

Strewn across the Velika Planina, a mile-high plateau, weathered cottages shelter herders and their cattle

summering on the rich meadows. From here eastward, the Alps lose their majesty, settling into rolling hills.

assault of Grintovca; Franc, with a day of haying before him, waved and turned for home. In a steep three-hour hike, four herds passed me when I paused for breath, each animal seeming to cast a disdainful glance my way.

Three-quarters of the way to the top of Grintovca, we came to the pasture—a steep treeless meadow scattered with a dozen rough cabins. One served as the cheese-making center for the summer community.

As tired cattle set to the sweet grass, 50-year-old Valentin Gartner of Studor summarized his summer-long job: "I milk my seven cows at 4 a.m. and 5 p.m., then spend the rest of the day making cheese." Inside the shed, he showed me the 3½-foot-wide copper kettle he puts over a wood fire to heat the milk, the strainer he uses to skim off the curds, and the 2-foot-wide wooden rounds in which the cheese solidifies.

After a lunch of bread and the creamy-white Bohinj cheese Mr. Gartner makes, I sat in a field of daisies, columbines, and buttercups, picking tart wild strawberries as the cattle lazed and chewed their cuds.

In late afternoon, I descended Grintovca and returned to Franc's house in Studor, a small village of 45 farm families nestled in a glacier-carved valley near Lake Bohinj.

I first saw Studor and the Cveteks on a cold, misty February day. A chill rain softened the packed snow that in winter forms pathways in the village and I tramped through this slush into the Cveteks' courtyard. On the left stood the barn—shelter for cows, pigs, chickens, sheep, and a horse— and on the right the two-story house, firewood stacked neatly beside the plastered wall.

Franc greeted me at the door as I wiped the snow from my boots on the *predpražnik*, a doormat of braided corn stalks. He ushered me into the humid kitchen, warmed by a wood stove. With Franc and his wife, Špela, live two married daughters, Tilka and Ivanka, and their families. We all crowded into the kitchen as Tilka served the homemade plum brandy they call *slivovka* and a kind of paste called *zaska*, pork fat, bacon, and garlic that is spread on toast.

Talking and working with the Cveteks in February and in June, I learned that they are in a time of transition, a transition that takes

Rimmed by tumbled ridges, Lake Bled sparkles in fading sunlight; boats creep past the baroque church on the lake's only island.

two forms: the first in the daily functioning of the farm, the second in its economic base.

Many chores are still performed in the traditional way; but modern methods are making inroads. Franc was breaking in a young ox to pull hay carts even though he owns a small tractor. In the hayfields, he wields a scythe in a long fluid arc—but a gasoline-powered blade mows faster. The family sometimes drives a horse-drawn cart although they own a car and a motorbike.

A PROSPEROUS FARMER, Franc Cvetek owns no more arable land than anyone else. "The government permits each farmer to own 10 hectares [about 25 acres]. Since we have three families in our house, we have 30 hectares." We were wandering through Studor, snow crunching beneath our feet. In the distance, wooden racks for drying and storing hay stood out starkly as if brushed on the snow by a Japanese calligrapher. I asked where his land was and he pointed in several directions. "We plant vegetables—corn, carrots, potatoes—here in a garden near the village. I have hayfields near the lake and grazing meadows in the planinas. Our land is in small patches in various places because the farmers share good and bad land. But we all still need more."

That second, and more profound, change may eventually lead the Cveteks away from their farming life. "Today, farming alone cannot support the family as it did in the past," Franc stated. So other sources of income are needed. For instance, Anton Taler, a son-in-law, works full-time at a sawmill, helping with farm chores evenings and weekends.

But the growth of tourism has brought the greatest change. Tourists—mostly German and Dutch—have begun to flock to Lake Bohinj, a small pristine lake two and a half miles long. Surrounded by cliffs, lined by trees and beaches, this lake is basically undeveloped, with only a few hotels and guesthouses at its shores. The Cveteks own three rentable houses and each requires a heavy investment of time and money.

Franc's 25-year-old son Jože manages the houses but also helps with haying and other farm work. Jože and his wife—both university graduates—teach at a local public school in winter; but during the summer season, they devote their time to vacationists.

To finance the construction of the new guesthouse, Franc sold several cattle—a major decision. Jože showed me through the

Cut by three roiling rivers—the Soča, Sava Dolinka, and Sava Bohinjka—the mountain ranges of Slovenia thrust craggy limestone heads into the clouds, a final convulsion of splendor before the Alps trail eastward into foothills. Mountaineers prize the ruggedness of the Julian Alps; tourists admire the sweeping beauty of Lake Bled and Lake Bohinj.

house; each of the seven bright, clean rooms was furnished with new beds and built-in closets and four had private baths.

One day as we sat in a *gostilna*—a tavern —near the guesthouse, Franc asserted that "the farm is still the base of everything. Politics and economics can quickly influence the tourist trade, but the farm will always be the stable foundation—and tourists need the milk, cheese, and butter that the farm provides." I asked whether one of his grandchildren would eventually own the farm. He quickly and emphatically replied. "Yes, someone will always care for the farm—it has been in the family for over 200 years."

Just then, one of the youngsters burst in and announced that some new guests had arrived—Germans, he thought. "During World War I when I was a young man," Franc said, chuckling, "Hungarian soldiers were quartered in Studor and I learned to count in their language. During World War II, I had to learn some German. Now we have our own country and my family must learn words in several languages to speak with tourists."

Slovenia has had just that kind of history— a history of conquest and foreign domination. It was part of a sovereign nation only once before the establishment of Yugoslavia in 1918—and that was more than 1,300 years ago when Samo, a Slavonic king, organized an empire that lasted a brief 31 years. The Slovenes—a Slavic tribe—had migrated from the east, settling in the Sava River valley in the last part of the sixth century.

For the five centuries after 750, the Slovenes were ruled by the Frankish and the Holy Roman Empires. In the 13th century, the Habsburg dynasty gained control, and with one interruption, held sway until World War I.

From the 15th to the 17th centuries, Turkish armies passed through Gorenjska, raiding farms and villages. To warn of these invaders, Slovenes used mountaintop bonfires; the people then gathered in a protected area, usually a fortified church.

On a steaming July day, I visited Crngrob, a massive Gothic church that the Turks raided in the late 1400's. Perched on a low knoll, it overlooks the broad Sava Valley and the medieval city of Kranj. Marija Maserl, 70-year-old caretaker of the church, unlocked its heavy, carved door with a six-inch key. And with one glance, I understood what drew the Turks to this edifice: paintings, gilt statues, ornate gold altarpieces.

"On the day of the attack—we don't know exactly when it was—the farmers from the countryside came here," Marija explained as we walked through the cool nave. Bright eyes sparkled as she narrated the story for the uncounted hundredth time. "After a fierce fight, the small party of Turks breached the eight-foot wall and one horseman broke into the church. The peasants clustered at the altar praying to the Holy Mother; as the Turk galloped toward them, Mary answered their prayers: A hole opened in the floor and swallowed horse and rider, but not before the animal left a hoofprint in the rock floor of the church." Understandably enough, the other Turks fled. To prove the story, Marija showed me a two-foot-square block of stone marked with a small Arabian sized horseshoe print.

The next major incursion into Slovenia occurred from a different direction and produced different results. Napoleon marched through in 1797, 1800, 1805, and 1809, finally annexing Slovenia and nearby territories. In the Illyrian Provinces of the French Empire, the Slovenes enjoyed an interlude of freedom from Habsburg rule, with administrative and legal reform. In 1815, however, after Napoleon's last defeat, the Congress of Vienna restored them to the Habsburgs.

The 20th-century history of Gorenjska—except for the last 20 years—is a complex mixture of war, foreign domination, and troubled national government. One morning near the Predel pass at the Italian border, I talked to an old woman who summarized her country's recent past. As she weeded a small patch of potatoes, she said, "I was born an Austrian, grew up an Italian, and will die a Yugoslav—and I have never left my home."

During World War I, Slovenes were drafted into the Austrian army and a major campaign against Italian troops was waged on what today is Slovenian soil. This theater of war from 1915 to 1917 was the Soča River—the Isonzo to Italians—and the culminating battle was at Caporetto—Kobarid to Slovenes. A young American ambulance driver served with the Italians, recording part of the experience in *A Farewell to Arms*.

"In the bed of the river there were pebbles and boulders, dry and white in the sun, and the water was clear and swiftly moving and blue in the channels," wrote Ernest Hemingway of the Soča. More than half a century later, it retains its pure aspect—an aquamarine ribbon pirouetting over and around rocks the color of milk. After months of battle near the river, the Germans and Austrians in 1917 launched a surprise attack that drove the Italians out of the Soča Valley.

Peace treaties in 1919 acknowledged the Kingdom of the Serbs, Croats, and Slovenes, later renamed Yugoslavia—Land of the South Slavs. Slovenia lost the Soča Valley—almost entirely Slavic—to Italy, and did not regain it until after the next war. That war struck Yugoslavia on April 6, 1941, when Hitler's *Wehrmacht* invaded.

Just three weeks later, the *Osvobodilna Fronta (OF)*, the Slovene Liberation Front, was organized—the first such resistance group in occupied Europe. The guerrillas, mostly young men, lived in small bands in the mountains, striking bridges, railroads, and truck convoys at night. By 1942, the OF had become part of the Communist resistance organization led by Josip Broz Tito.

MORE THAN a quarter century after the war's end, its memory still flickers: in the wreath of fresh flowers on a Partisan's grave, in the village plaque or sculpture dedicated to the fallen. But the most poignant monument lies in the small town of Begunje, huddled near the Karavanke. The Gestapo transformed an old castle into a prison for captured Partisans and other Slovenes; one wing is kept as a museum, the wing that contained cells for the condemned. More than 12,000 men, women, and children were interned at Begunje; 849 were executed there.

The cells were cold and somber the winter day I visited them. The deepest chill spread from words inscribed on cell walls by Slovenes: "I'll always remember you darling"; "You never know where death is waiting"; "To our companions, revenge us."

I heard the living voice of war's tragedy in the tiny village of Strmec, high above the Soča River. In October 1943, Partisans raided a convoy at Strmec, killing two Germans; in reprisal, German troops shot 16 villagers. I talked to 85-year-old Helena Vencelj, whose husband and sons were among those executed. Framed in the doorway of her white plaster house, she recalled the events of that day. Her face wrinkled and careworn, her eyes red and brimming with tears, she said: "They shot the men at dawn and then burned the village. The other women and I escaped, but we vowed to wear black until we died." Mrs. Vencelj wore a black blouse; a black scarf covered a shock of white hair. "After the war, Americans gave us money to rebuild the town, but today only 11 families live here—in the old days, we had over 200."

At the southern extremity of the Julian Alps I heard a different echo from the war. Bolnica Franja, a Partisan hospital, consists of rough frame buildings tucked in the gorge of a fast-moving stream. By chance, a group of 200 former Partisans was visiting Bolnica Franja the day I went there; and in their number was Dr. Victor Volčjak, one of the hospital's founders. Tall and thin with a crown of white hair, Dr. Volčjak told me, "The Germans tried to attack us several times; but because we were hidden in the gorge, and fought back, they failed. The hospital worked until the liberation in 1945."

After touring the hospital, the Partisans—men from all over Yugoslavia—joined in the *kolo,* a national dance. Linking arms, they chanted songs recalling war deeds and extolling Tito, sometimes dancing in a circle, sometimes in a chain snaking around each other. Their exuberance was contagious, and I found myself clapping and shouting with them. That Partisan spirit contributed to the establishment of the new Yugoslavia, today a prosperous nation of 20 million people—of whom one-tenth are Slovenes.

Woven in the fabric of Slovene history is the thread of its literature. Today, the republic has one of the highest literacy rates in the world—virtually 100 percent—and a saying that goes: "One Slovene, a publishing house; two Slovenes, a literary society; three Slovenes, a second publishing house."

In 1551, Primož Trubar, a Protestant clergyman, published a catechism in Slovene—the first work to use the local language. Others soon followed—hymnbooks, the Bible, a grammar—but this interlude of literary freedom was soon squelched by the Counter-Reformation.

Under Napoleon, Slovene became an official language and publishing flourished again. Into this turmoil of change one of the great heroes of Slovene literature was born—the Romantic poet Franc Prešeren.

I was introduced to Prešeren's poetry in the backyard orchard of Franc Pikelj—a retired schoolteacher and devotee of Prešeren's—in Radovljica, an old town on the east bank of the Sava. As billowing clouds built into a summer thundershower and his grandchildren, high in the trees, dropped fresh cherries for us to eat, Mr. Pikelj told me of the poet's life and works. "Like most Romantic poets, Prešeren lived a turbulent life —poverty, tragic love affairs, and illegitimate children haunted him. But that seemed to add to the sensitiveness of his poetry." In a rich baritone, Mr. Pikelj read his favorite poem, "Vrba," named for Prešeren's home at the foot of the Karavanke. Thunder from the impending storm—"just the setting for a Romantic poet," Mr. Pikelj commented— punctuated the words as he read: "To thee, sweet, happy Vrba, all my praise!/Dear corner of my father's home and land,/Why did the thirst for knowledge e'er demand/My going hence into life's tortuous ways...."

A POUNDING RAIN soon demanded my going hence but I returned to Radovljica the next day to visit Matej Bor, a poet whose first book, *Let Us Outstorm the Storm,* was published clandestinely during World War II. A burly man with a graying fringe of hair, Matej Bor speaks in a breathless, serious way—but is quick to laugh. Besides lyric and epic poetry, he has written plays, a novel, criticism, and is currently completing a new translation of Shakespeare's plays.

Over a glass of white wine, we talked of poetry. "The best of Slovenian poetry is as good as the best from other countries," he told me. "The only difference is that our poetry is written in a small, unfamiliar language, and one that is rarely spoken or translated out of our country."

Of his own poetry, he said, "I am a man who writes about himself and about man's place on the planet." Intensely concerned over pollution, Matej Bor is chairman of an environmental protection association. "We don't have the ecological problems some areas do, but still there are evidences of deterioration."

Like their counterparts the world over, Slovenia's poets are inspired by natural beauty. Of Lake Bled, Prešeren wrote: "... this lake to me a paradise doth seem...." His words ring true to me, in spite of tour buses belching exhaust fumes or workers wielding jackhammers at Bled, major tourist center

of Gorenjska. A glacial lake of emerald waters, only a mile and a half long, Bled snuggles among small green mountains with Triglav towering to the northwest. Lake Bled is so popular that within a fortnight I saw three heads of state—President Tito, Emperor Haile Selassie of Ethiopia, and President V. V. Giri of India—more dignitaries than I see in a year in my native Washington, D. C.

Centrally located in the Slovenian Alps, Bled makes an excellent headquarters for exploring Gorenjska. One morning I visited the man who makes all the cow and sheep bells for the area. "Each bell has a different sound and I can identify every one I make," Vinko Jan told me, sitting in the shop where his family has made bells by hand for more than 500 years.

On another day I watched Alojz Lotrič of Gorjuse carve intricate smoking pipes from pearwood—a trade he learned from his grandfather and father.

Soot-covered and dressed in black, a chimney sweep sipped a glass of wine in a gostilna. "Yes, my father taught me this job," he said, "but I'm retired now—I only cleaned 22 chimneys today."

One of my lingering memories of Bled is the afternoon I spent with Ivan Dobnikar, a retired shopkeeper whose lifelong hobby has been bees. I asked him if he, too, had learned this from his father. "No," he replied, "I taught him." Slovenia has a long tradition of beekeeping, and a museum in Radovljica is the only one anywhere dedicated to the apiary arts. "Our *kranjska sivka* bee is a hardy, adaptable strain," Mr. Dobnikar said, "and it is exported everywhere in the world."

I accompanied Mr. Dobnikar to his backyard bee house—a seven-foot-tall wooden structure containing ten hives. Each hive had a colorfully painted door with a slit for the bees to come and go; each bee knows its home hive by the arrangement of colors. As I admired the doors, one of Mr. Dobnikar's 800,000 bees took a dislike to me; it chased me around the yard, became entangled in my hair, and finally stung me on the neck. Perhaps to soothe me, Mr. Dobnikar offered some of his honey. Thick, rich, and dark, it tasted of the essence of sweetness. "In a good year, I harvest almost 650 pounds," Mr. Dobnikar said. He pondered my final question with a smile. "If I were a bee, I would choose the life of the plain, simple worker."

In Kropa, a small town tucked in a steep valley, I met another man who leads a simple life. Crouched by a smoldering charcoal fire, 74-year-old Daniel Šolar heated a spike red-hot; when it reached the right temperature he swung it to an anvil, hammered it into shape, and within a minute presented me with a delicately twisted nail, ready for the hinge of a door. As he worked, he told me, "For generations, Kropa has had master iron-workers—we made nails, candle holders, and ornate grillwork for the Habsburgs and for Slovenia. Now, our work is mainly for tourists." A dozen visitors crowded into Mr. Šolar's shop, appropriately named Purgatory.

Small and frail-looking, Mr. Šolar was not my idea of an ironworker, but across the street I met a man who was. Joža Bertoncelj —swarthy, muscular, barrel-chested—is one of Gorenjska's foremost artists in iron. "I have to be strong," he said, "some of my statues weigh hundreds of pounds." One of his most famous works is a memorial at Ljubelj, a Nazi concentration camp: an iron skeleton reaching skyward with manacled hands, its mouth gaping in an agonized scream. "We feel a strong duty to those who suffered and died in those years," said Božidar Štolcar, my 61-year-old interpreter.

BUT MEMORIALS to the past are not the only obligations Slovenians feel, I found out. One winter afternoon, I walked along the shore of Lake Bled with a Slovene friend, Marijan Jarc. Snow-clad Triglav stood clear in the distance; I asked if he had ever climbed it.

"Oh yes," he exclaimed, "every Slovene feels a moral obligation to climb Triglav at least once in his life. I was five years old on my first trip." To understand Slovenes better, I decided, I must climb Triglav.

At six o'clock one bright July morning our party drove from Bled to Rudno Polje, the jumping-off point for our three-day trek. Accompanying me were my wife, Linda, Mr. Štolcar, and a Slovene photographer, Jaka Čop. Jaka has published several books of photographs of the Julian Alps and I was honored that he agreed to guide us.

As we drove across a broad tree-lined plateau, I asked Mr. Štolcar how many times he had climbed Triglav. His answer, seven, impressed me until I asked Jaka: "This will be my 113th climb," he said. But even that paled in comparison to Matija Klinar, a mountain of a man I met later, who claimed to have reached Triglav's top 265 times— almost once for each of his 300 pounds.

We shouldered our packs at Rudno Polje

and immediately began the first steep climb. "We must go slowly and carefully," Jaka warned. At a deliberate pace, we climbed steadily for two hours, reaching a field of flowers and grass where we paused for a snack of cheese and peaches. Rested, we tackled the next climb and were soon rewarded with a vista of Lake Bohinj and the high meadow on Grintovca where I had climbed with the cattle just three weeks before.

Skirting Tošč, a humpbacked mountain garlanded with wild flowers, we met Triglav fullface. From a distance, I can dispassionately consider mountains. Up close, however, I tend to be more emotional; Triglav seemed a massive, foreboding Gargantua. I recalled the words of Julius Kugy, a Slovene who loved climbing the Julian Alps: "Triglav is not a mountain. It is a kingdom."

An hour's hike brought us to Vodnikova Koča for a bracing lunch of beef broth, lemonade, and bread. The Slovenian Alps are dotted with such koče—cabins—where climbers may buy a meal or rent a bed. As we sipped čaj, a supersweet tea, a group of young hikers puffed in, the stoutest man carrying a girl grimacing with pain—one knee was bandaged and a foot hung loosely. "We were near the summit," she said, "when a rock gave out under me. I must have fallen 25 feet." A disquieting story.

We left Vodnikova Koča and passed high above Velo Polje—loftiest summer meadow in the Julian Alps. There Linda saw a shape like a deer; Jaka told us it was a chamois. "But it's old and about to die or else it would be hiding at this time of day.

"We have a legend about Zlatorog, a white chamois with golden horns. He lived on Triglav and a hunter one day wounded him after a long chase. From the blood sprang a red flower that Zlatorog ate, healing him. He then turned on the hunter and forced him off a cliff. That red flower may be the wild carnation—the emblem of Slovenia."

Sunlight was fading and the night chill setting in as we reached Dom Planika, our overnight koča. Built of limestone and perched on a bald hump of rock, Planika seemed an extension of the mountain, Triglav, almost close enough to touch, soared above us.

Dawn found us chasing sleep with a cup of čaj. We left Planika in a plume of cloud that played tag with us the entire morning— now shrouding us, now dissipating to reveal distant ranges and valleys. The route took us up a steep snowbank; digging the edges of

Corroding cannon points across the mist-shrouded Soča Valley near Kobarid (Caporetto), in World War I a battleground disputed by Italian and Austrian-German forces. Dancing a kolo, *former Yugoslav Partisans chant songs honoring deeds of their resistance movement during World War II. In 1918 Slovenia became part of a new and independent Yugoslav state; for the previous millennium it had survived under foreign sovereignty.*

our boots in, we angled our way to its top. From there, we scampered and clambered over rocks and up ridgelines to the top of Mali Triglav, a minor summit 450 feet below Triglav. Iron cables and spikes secured to the rocks helped us through the more difficult places. From Mali Triglav the trail followed a narrow ridge with cliffs dropping hundreds of feet on either side. Our elusive cloud chose that moment to envelop us, making the footing even more treacherous. Within 20 minutes, however, we approached the summit and the cloud split apart, yielding a regal view of Gorenjska.

Jaka hugged Linda, shook my hand, and administered the three traditional spanks for any first-timer atop Triglav. We then drifted apart with our own thoughts, I with the same surging exultation that overtakes me at the top of any mountain.

The clouds scudded gently together again and we started the long descent to Lake Bohinj—gratified at conquering our first Alp.

On one of my last summer days in Gorenjska, I boarded a cable car to Velika Planina, a rolling plateau high in the Kamniške Alps. I counted dozens of ski chalets at its western edge; and the pounding of hammers and the chugging grind of a rock crusher signaled the construction of more.

As I wandered through this bustling new community, I reflected on the Slovenian people I had met. During a millennium of foreign domination, these sturdy, patient Slavs had managed to retain their unique identity and language and to stitch together a culture that survived the stormiest of times. And now, part of their own nation, the Slovenes are free to compete with neighboring countries—countries that once ruled them. A true testament to a steadfast people, I thought.

The grumbling of the rock crusher faded as I climbed across Velika Planina. I sat on a jagged rock at the edge of an escarpment, looking at the easternmost ranges of the Alps as they tapered into faraway valleys. A mist gathered below me and gradually climbed upward. Drifting through low cuts in the ridge, it carpeted the meadows behind me where cattle summering on the plateau were grazing. The cloud crept slowly higher, wisping past me at first, but finally wrapping my rock and me in an impermanent curtain the texture of sea foam. Completely obscured, I could discern only the clamor of cowbells and the forlorn bawl of a calf separated from its mother. □

HANS, A GRAVE-LOOKING BOY of six, trudged into the room hugging two round loaves of bread. He dropped them with a heavy thud on top of the bin for the firewood.

Frau Thurner quartered an onion and handed him a piece, saying, "I'll tell Christkindl you are a good boy."

Hans nibbled on the onion and counted the days to Christmas Eve when Christkindl, the Christ Child, would come with gifts. Then he ran to join his little brother, Toni, and his sisters, Maresi and Barbara. They were helping their father in the smokehouse, where the family usually stored the month's supply of homemade bread. Anton Thurner was threading chunks of pork onto long metal rods to fit in the oven where the meat would smoke for four days. As they worked, the father, a lean, taciturn mountain man, reminded the children how good the smoked bacon would taste in the months to come.

I was sitting in the large warm kitchen of an Austrian farmhouse near the village of Wagrain. Just a few days before, in Washington, I had received a message relayed by the Austrian Embassy: "The family Thurner welcomes you, and is pleased to have you join them for Christmas."

"Herzlich Willkommen"—a heartfelt welcome—greeted me again and again: in vaulted castles, in towns along fast-flowing rivers, on mountain meadows, and at inns where easygoing hospitality lingers far into the night.

My travels led me in and out of valleys in the keen chill of winter fog, the beauty of a mountain world lit by sun and snow. I returned in summer driving on arrow-straight autobahns and abrupt, heart-stopping roads that loop and twist around and through the mountains that dominate most of Austria. I spent weeks roaming the Austrian ranges, which rise in the west above Lake Constance and taper away 300 miles to the east outside Vienna into the plains bordering Hungary. And everywhere I encountered the same hearty, spontaneous friendliness that adds a special grace to the tourist trade—Austria's most rapidly growing industry.

My journeys began a few days before Christmas as I headed south from Salzburg, a city on the *(Continued on page 193)*

In a candlelight program of carols, stories, and prayer, a third-grade class celebrates Christmas in the Alpine village of Wagrain.

8

Austria: Village Idyll and Festive Towns

By CYNTHIA RUSS RAMSAY
Photographs by GEORGE F. MOBLEY

Drama of salvation: as performed in Salzburg, Death in a black cape comes to claim Jedermann—Everyman, rich and frivolous. Mammon, webbed in gold, scorns Jedermann as a prisoner of his possessions. Good Deeds, pale and feeble, struggles to rise to her knees to help Jedermann called before the judgment seat of God. Staged outdoors before the great cathedral, Hugo von Hofmannsthal's 20th-century morality play has become a permanent feature of the famous summer festival. Year after year, each Sunday during the season, The Salzburg Everyman *reminds its audience "How our earthly days and deeds/Are transitory and full of needs."*

Gleaming in floodlight, Salzburg's baroque churches dominate the city; twin spires identify the cathedral. On a

hill above stands the massive Hohensalzburg fortress. Ribbons of light trace traffic along the Salzach River.

Sleek Lipizzaner stallions frolic on the rolling meadows of the Piber stud farm near the city of Graz in Styria. Since the 16th century the Spanish Riding School in Vienna has trained the carefully bred horses in such stately and difficult maneuvers as the poised leap called the capriole. Skirting the peaks around Zell am See, a sailplane stays safely aloft by riding the air currents that rise along mountain ridges. The swift current, sharp rocks, and churning waters of the Lech River make kayaking a more dangerous sport.

Before a marble-and-gold altar, German Vesko and Trude Mühr take their marriage vows in the parish church of Bad Aussee, a small Styrian resort town. Friends of the bridegroom, a petroleum engineer, designed the "oil rig" as a surprise gift to spout beer for the wedding party and guests.

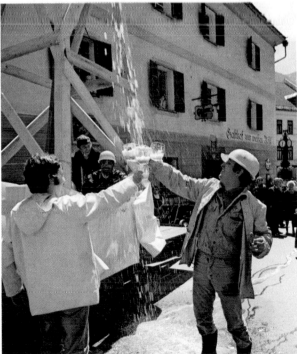

Lunch hour in Salzburg brings carriages to a halt; horses munch their oats and a coachman slakes his thirst after taking sightseers through the city. These tours by Fiaker pass churches, palaces, and formal gardens built by powerful prince-archbishops who ruled Salzburg for a thousand years. In the evening a blond singer performs at a Restaurant-Café. At Holzgau, a Tyrolean community of 386 high in the Lech Valley, villagers read and gossip in the afternoon sun, turning their backs on the make-believe façade of the house that contains municipal offices. Fresco creates the illusion of three-dimensional stonework in lavish baroque ornament.

Knife-edge ridges and sharp peaks get their shape from erosion by glaciers, rivers of ice inching downhill. The

GERHARD KLAMMET

Wildspitze Glacier, relic of the last Ice Age, deepens a valley between granite summits of Tyrol's Ötztaler Alps.

Contemporary design and traditional skill distinguish a glass figure — photographed in polarized light for quality-control analysis — and wrought-iron chessmen. In a forge at Kitzbühel, a blacksmith hammers red-hot iron into a flower; by similar techniques his medieval and Renaissance predecessors made fine armor. At nearby Rattenberg, a glass-cutting center, a nucleus of light in the blue dusk reveals a shopkeeper among fragile crystal. Austria's craftsmen also work in leather, porcelain, silver, enamel, lace. Petit point adorns handbags or jewelry. These luxury items, all handmade, account for 15 percent of the value of Austrian exports.

In the revelry of Fasching, Austria's long Carnival season, party-goers in mod costumes pause demurely for a kiss. More classic in dress, a weary clown slumps in her chair as the pace of merrymaking slows near daybreak. This hectic round of pre-Lenten balls and parades begins about mid-January and ends on Ash Wednesday. Dating from the Middle Ages, the custom of carousing in disguise formerly meant that men of different guilds or rank—nobles and commoners—could mingle without embarrassment.

On Palm Sunday morning, worshipers ascend the slopes above the town of Thaur to reach a hill top chapel. A small bystander clutches a gay umbrella during a shower. Nearly 90 percent of Austrians profess the faith of Roman Catholicism, keeping the holidays of the church but also enjoying colorful local festivals that hark back to pagan times. In Perchten processions, marchers wearing lovely masks or ugly ones symbolize the victory of good over evil — and of spring over winter.

northern edge of the Alps. It was an opulent, glittering winter day. Snow dappled the pines; ice crusted the larches; icicles dripped from timbered, gabled roofs — all was flash and sparkle in the dazzling sunlight.

"You've come in time to see the Thurners decorate their tree," said Astrid Gruber of Wagrain's Tourist Office. "Last week the children went with their father to cut the tree from the family's forest on the slopes behind their house. But," Astrid explained, "it was only to help the Christ Child."

We were driving down the village main street on the way to the Thurners'. Pine boughs garlanded the wooden balconies, spilling out of flowerboxes that in summer bloom bright red with geraniums.

"Remember," cautioned Astrid as we entered the Thurners' yellow stucco house, "it is the Christ Child who trims the tree." But the children were already fast asleep.

Barbara Thurner, an apple-cheeked woman of 32 with thick braids wound around her head, ushered me into the *Stube,* a cozy parlor with beamed ceilings that had witnessed the joys of Christmas for more than 300 years. A bench adjoined the barrel-shaped stove filling one corner of the room. I sat there, barely out of the way, and watched the glistening ornaments work their magic. The Thurners told me of St. Nicholas and Krampus as they clipped candies, sparklers, and candles to the slender branches.

The holiday season begins with the visit of St. Nicholas on the eve of his birthday, December 6. He goes from house to house bringing cookies, fruits, and nuts to the good children. The bad are at the mercy of Krampus, a fierce and frightening figure; he wears a black mask with devil's horns and a huge, protruding red tongue; and when he makes the rounds with St. Nicholas he wields a bundle of switches. Fortunately, the misdeeds of the Thurner children were few, and they escaped the sting of the *Ruten.*

Soon the tree stood resplendent in holiday finery, awaiting only the final touches of lustrous fibers of angel's hair.

"Don't unravel the skeins," said Frau Thurner. "Leave it twisted together as it is, as if Christkindl had left a little bit of his hair."

On the day we were all waiting for, patches

Always in fashion: An Innsbruck girl models the dirndl. Details of cut or trim in this popular folk dress vary from region to region.

of fog hung over the village, peaks disappeared into the clouds, the pines on the lower slopes looked black in the cold light of a leaden sky. But as dusk descended, the lights of Christmas banished the gloom. I could see rows of tiny trees trimmed with tinsel and flickering candles in the church cemetery as Astrid and I hurried by, hoping we were not too late to see the children and Heini Ganschitter, a farmhand, carry the Christmas incense through the house and barn. We were in plenty of time, for this ritual blessing of each room and building had to wait until the cows had been milked and the hogs and chickens fed.

The children, up from their afternoon nap, sprawled on the kitchen floor drinking milk from baby bottles — "preschool bottles" here. "The children have three bottles a day until they start school," Frau Thurner remarked. She was already dressed in a holiday dirndl of brocade with a pink silken apron.

By the time Anton Thurner finished his chores, the savory aroma of bratwurst and sauerkraut filled the room and a big pot of *Knödel* (dumplings) simmered on the stove.

SUDDENLY, an angel with curly blond hair and a paper crown burst into the room and began to chant in a high, sweet voice. As the little girl sang, a woman with a shawl draped over her head, and three men filed in. The *Herbersuche* had begun. This time-honored folk pageant, performed from house to house, re-enacts the search for shelter at Bethlehem. Mary and Joseph were unmistakable; the man in red fez and white apron was obviously the innkeeper. "But who," I whispered, "is the man in rags and tatters?"

Astrid murmured her reply: "The beggarman who symbolizes the poverty of Christ."

As Joseph began to plead with the innkeeper to open his doors, Frau Thurner lit the white Christmas candle. When the brief play ended, artists and audience broke into a lively chatter before a spread of apples, cookies, and wine.

"Not another drop." The innkeeper raised his hands as Anton Thurner tried to fill the glasses one more time. "We have many stops to make." And amid a flurry of hugs, handshakes, and warm wishes of *Fröhliche Weihnachten* — Merry Christmas — the players left us to our supper.

Her face glowing with happiness, Barbara Thurner knelt in prayer with her children. Then a tinkle of bells in the corridor brought

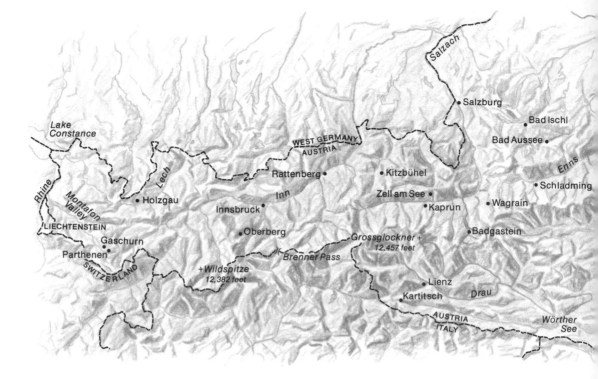

Mountains dominate rugged Austria, realm of one-third of all the Alps. The Austrian ranges extend from Lake Constance and the Swiss frontier in the west to the doorsteps of Vienna more than 300 miles to the east. In the gentle hills of the Vienna Woods, final outposts of the Alps, this mighty chain of mountains subsides at last into plainsland.

cries of exultation from all. "Christkindl has come!" The children jiggled impatiently as their mother tried to comb their hair. Solemnly and somewhat awed, the children opened the door to the stube, locked for so many days, and saw the tree shining with the radiance of candlelight.

Barbara wouldn't let go of her doll's cradle. The boys wanted to take their new tractors to bed with them. Maresi tried to take a second candy from the tree, but was reminded that the sweets had to last a month.

Much later that night, bells pealed through the valley, splintering the silence. Then the only sound was the crunch of footsteps on the crusty snow as the faithful flocked to the steepled church.

On another evening that same week, I listened to the sound of folk music—the robust footstamping, handclapping melodies of the *Schuhplattler*—shoe-slapping dances.

Young men in lederhosen and girls in dirndls twirled to the rhythms of an accordion, xylophone, and zither.

"I arranged this *Heimatabend*—Folk Evening—with the help and participation of the local people," said Astrid Gruber. "Wagrain has so many visitors at this season we all work together to keep them amused."

Wagrain, I learned, like so many Alpine villages, prospers on tourism in winter as well as summer. In winter the big attraction is skiing, and there is hardly a mountain village without a ski lift nearby.

"As recently as 1958 Wagrain was a poor farming village," Astrid told me, "but at that time people turned to tourism as the key to prosperity.

"In those early days Wagrain didn't have machines to pack the snow on the *pistes*—the ski runs. Instead, in church on Sundays the priest would call for volunteers—'*Pistenkommando*'—to prepare the slopes for the tourists. What a game they made of side-stepping up the mountains to stamp the snow down with their skis."

Community spirit also played a role in the development of the Montafon Valley in Vorarlberg, Austria's westernmost province.

"Each family volunteered to give a day's labor a year to help cut paths up the mountains to attract hikers and mountain climbers in summer," said Arthur Kessler, owner of the Posthotel Rössle in the resort village of Gaschurn. As we talked, Herr Kessler showed me the hotel guestbook with entries dating from 1870. In early years nearly everybody signed the book with a verse or two. "People were more romantic then." There was a tinge of nostalgia in his voice. Still....

"In those days poverty drove many of the men from the valley in search of jobs. With the first snows of winter the men returned to their families with the money earned as masons and plasterers," he recalled.

But the rumble of bulldozers and concrete mixers has come to the valley, and most Montafoners stay at home, taking part in their own building boom.

The Montafon Valley owes its good fortune to the mountains, for the sharp granite peaks and high ridges can bestow more than their blessing of beauty. Tamed somewhat, they attract winter sports enthusiasts in ever-increasing numbers, and they bring the bounty of hydroelectric power.

From Gaschurn I followed the Ill, a swift and shallow Alpine stream, to Partenen, the last village at the head of the valley. I went to see power produced inside a mountain. The river there carved such a narrow cleft that to build a power plant the engineers had to tunnel deep into the mountainside.

Six other power stations strung out along the Ill also harness the energy born in the snow and ice, sleet and rain, glaciers and lakes of the Silvretta range.

It is these same mountains of the Silvretta, along with the Rhätikon chain to the west, that form the major watershed of Central Europe. This great bulge of peaks and wind-swept crags divides the restless Alpine rivers between the Danube and the Rhine.

Sometimes the waters of the Alps also carry the promise of vigor regained and health restored. Scores of spas scattered throughout the region treat guests or patients "taking the cure" with the waters of mineral or thermal springs.

I talked to Dr. Alois Ringl about the remedies offered at Badgastein, an elegant spa and resort where luxury amid crystal and candlelight provides its own therapy.

"Generally we use the waters from our 14 springs for thermal baths, drinking cures, and underwater massage," said Dr. Ringl, a specialist in internal medicine. "Every year thousands of ailing people from all over the world come here to get rid of their troubles and pains. I know very well that American doctors generally do not believe in balneology—using natural mineral and thermal waters for medical purposes—but it is a scientifically proved fact that many ailments are treated with good results with our waters. Our thermal baths are indicated for cases of chronic rheumatic diseases, high blood pressure, premature signs of aging, and insufficiencies of the endocrine glands."

Other Austrian spas—and there are more than a hundred—use sulphur, iodine, brine, or alkaline waters for remedies.

Whether or not the waters heal, Badgastein offers the visitor an unlikely blend of cosmopolitan comfort and the rugged outdoors.

It was a raw winter day when I turned into the Gastein Valley, which begins as a corridor between towering granite cliffs. Fog blurred the landscape in a phantom world of swirling mist and shadow shapes, but nothing, I think, could soften the stark wall of primitive rock looming above the narrow thread of road. Hunched over the wheel, I peered ahead on the alert for the next improbable bend or the yellow glimmer of an approaching car. I drove with the single-minded intensity of someone bent on survival.

The fog thinned suddenly, and a moment later I entered into an ocean of space. Tier after tier of snowclad peaks touched a flawless blue sky. Badgastein's palatial hotels lined the road—a miniature metropolis rising from the mist. It was the Land of Oz at the end of a difficult road.

Badgastein, a compact city of hotels, depends on tourism; but even tiny Oberberg, a hamlet of a few farms scattered on the slopes of a mountain 20 miles southwest of Innsbruck, seeks to attract vacationers in summer.

Anton Pfurtscheller and his brother Hans worked for six years building a new house that would accommodate guests in comfort, with running water and indoor plumbing. But the farm really lured city dwellers, mostly from Germany, as an island of tranquillity.

It was a short hike to the house from the gravel road below. As the roar of a river receded, I could hear the soft meadow sounds of crickets and bees rise up from the *Alm*—the sloping pastures that yield two harvests of hay each summer. Miniature daisies—flecks of white—tiny lavender bluebells and forget-me-nots, and pale dots of buttercups created a tapestry of subdued color on the mantle of green.

"Where the land is flat, we use tractors to

cut the grass," said Anton while he waited for his wife, Maria, to slice the bologna and cheese for supper. Translating for me was Eckart Söllner, a student from the University of Innsbruck.

"For most slopes we use motor mowers, but on certain steep sides we must still cut by hand. My brother and I help each other; and by the time we cut my fields and then his, my fields are ready for the second cutting. Everything is fixed right so I'll never have a day off," Anton said with a laugh and a shrug.

Later I learned that just the past Sunday Anton had spent several hours taking his guests on a walking tour in the mountains, near some of the Stubai glaciers.

"To make their stay more interesting," Maria confided.

Eckart had warned me that Maria, like many peasant women, would not talk much when her husband was present, but she was full of bright chatter otherwise. Once, with more than a little impatience, she told us that "one of the five other farmers around here wants to keep things the way they were when we all depended on just the land and our animals for our income. But with that he won't get to a higher standard of living.

"We have just three cows, three calves, and a few sheep and pigs—not half as many as we had before we started renting rooms."

I DON'T KNOW precisely how many hens they used to have, but there were enough still occupying the attic of the old house to create an eerie commotion in the ghostly hour before dawn. Strangely sharp rustling sounds had frightened me awake as I slept in one of the austere bedrooms on the floor below; and never having shared a house with laying hens I found those muted-but-oh-so-close noises rather disturbing.

Maria set a place for me at the family table in her big modern kitchen, and I greedily slathered sweet butter and rich jam on the crisp roll, a *Semmel*. This with coffee makes the continental breakfast that starts the day for many of the seven million Austrians. After feeding me, Maria proudly showed me a small wooden chest, carved and gaily painted in the bold floral motifs of Tyrolean folk art.

"My husband made 40 of these last winter. He does the cabinetwork, and then he takes them to a painter. We've already sold all but five. You would pay much more for them in the shops."

As smoothly as Anton turned his wood-working skill to profit, Maria used her skill as a housekeeper to take the summer wave of guests in her stride. Cooking, dishwashing, cleaning, and keeping track of all the extra soft drinks, beers, and snacks seemed simple enough as she coped with it.

"Does Maria mind all the extra work?" I asked Eckart. I could see that her own three children—none older than seven—had to wait for breakfast while she fed 18 guests.

"I don't mind," she smiled, trying to release her skirt from her son's fierce grip. "The winters are long and lonely enough, and I enjoy the company."

In winter the snowplow goes through regularly to clear a path for the valley jeep taking children to school in Neustift, the little town five miles away. Even when the family car could make the trip for her weekly marketing, Maria slides into Neustift on a sled. "Nothing can happen because the snow is piled high on both sides. You steer a little with the legs, and *es geht wunderbar.*" It is a less exciting trip, however, when Maria returns pulling her sledload of groceries—salt, sugar, sausages, fruit, vegetables—five miles uphill.

I gained additional perspective on rural life from Josef Bichler, spokesman for Tyrol's Department of Agriculture. "Like the Pfurtschellers, most Tyrolean farmers now make money from tourism. They used to be as self-sufficient as possible, and they would never specialize in just one thing as many do now. Traditionally they raise cattle or sheep, grow oats, barley, and other fodder, and harvest hay from the high meadows.

"Farmers can also log a small percentage of their forest with the permission of the federal government, if they promise to replant the trees within two years. But in Tyrol, and other provinces too, farmers increasingly rely on foreigners.

"A visitor once asked me," Herr Bichler added, chuckling, "why nearly every house in Austria is called 'Zimmer Frei.'" The little sign by the door or at the gate announces "Room for Rent," and paying guests have become a way of life.

For all its pastoral serenity, tiny Oberberg is just an hour's drive from Innsbruck, Tyrol's capital city, a leading university town and a scenic center of commerce.

Innsbruck owes its origins to the historic Brenner Pass, for it stands astride the most important north-south trade route across the Alps, linking northern Europe to Italy. Where German kings journeyed on narrow trails to the Pope in Rome for the crown of the Holy Roman Empire, trucks now speed along the Brenner autobahn, a major artery of the new and prosperous European Common Market.

At the hub of age-old traffic routes, Innsbruck offers the traveler hotels and inns with the special charm of Austrian *Gemütlichkeit*. At once exuberant and cosy, gemütlichkeit eludes definition until you find yourself sated with a hearty dinner, singing off-key, certain that, for the moment at least, this is the best of all possible worlds.

Herr Erwin Gutwinski, a dark-eyed man of unflagging energy, is heir to that tradition of innkeeping which takes pride in perfect service. He maintains a suave reticence until he decides to unleash an irreverent wit, and he manages both the Tyrol and the Europa hotels with an easy efficiency and an unrelenting commitment to high standards that he kept even during the last days of World War II.

"I was manager of the Oesterreichischer Hof in Salzburg when the U. S. 7th Army entered the city from Bavaria. It was May 4, 1945, and Brig. Gen. Robert N. Young ordered men of the Third Infantry Division to move into the hotel for a good rest," he told me. "In the evening they had the field kitchen outside on the street, but we served the meal with our fine china and silver. I had from the blackout small candles, and I put those on the table for a candlelight dinner.

"On that day I became a determined pacifist," he added. "As I looked at the young, pale, tired faces of the American troops I saw the faces of Germans and Austrians — just different helmets."

Parts of Innsbruck must look much as they did hundreds of years ago, with shoppers strolling in the shelter of Gothic arcades or along the broad boulevard of Maria-Theresien-Strasse lined with ornate 18th-century buildings in vivid tones of yellow, rose, apricot, and orange.

And always the spectacular panorama of craggy peaks. It seems to me nothing so shapes the character of Innsbruck as the dazzling wall of the Nordkette range above the northern edge of the city.

"I like to enjoy life, and that I can do only here with the mountains around," exclaimed Ulla Thien, energetic assistant to the mayor of Innsbruck. Ulla has lived in several European countries, but "I always return because of the mountains."

Sometimes it seems all 116,000 inhabitants are *am Berg,* an expression that means more than the literal translation of being in the mountains; it carries the significance of special involvement.

In summer I saw bleating sheep nudge picnickers in the meadows, 20 minutes above the city by funicular railway and swaying aerial tram. In winter this system lifts skiers from 1,900 to more than 7,700 feet. Students between classes, bureaucrats on their lunch hour, housewives in their spare time swoop down the steep flanks of the Hafelekar. At all seasons young and old find solitude and beauty on the mountain paths, in forest shade or open meadow.

THE "FOREST MILE" adds a new dimension to the mountain walk. Designed by physicians and promoted by a life-insurance company, this walk in the woods has thousands of people all over Austria swinging their arms, touching their toes, and chinning for health. The standard course has 20 stations with bright blue signs to explain the exercise at each stop; so many times for athletes, so many times for beginners, and how many times for me, I wondered, worn out before I was halfway through. These courses, first constructed in 1970, are appearing throughout Austria; and on any morning at all seasons but winter, you can see hundreds of people walking on the paths through the pinewoods, doing calisthenics with the songs of the birds to count by.

This enchantment with the outdoors, this enthusiasm for sports, find their best expression in the national pastime—skiing. But skiing is not merely a sport, it is a special communion with nature.

I make this assertion because, although I am one of those skiers who avoid the verticals—the tough ones—skiing is pure joy every time I do it. And summer skiing in Austria promised a bit of paradise.

A series of three cable cars carried me and crowds of other enthusiasts away from the village of Kaprun, above the timberline and beyond the intense wet green of the sedges. Airborne, we ascended the Kitzsteinhorn, near neighbor to the 12,457-foot Grossglockner, Austria's highest peak. I stepped out at 9,935 feet, just short of the top, into a white and gray landscape where the snow-covered expanse of glacier beckoned.

The sharp gleam of the glacier itself, gray-black with the rubble of gravel frozen in its depths, broke through the snow cover in menacing streaks here and there. . . .

I step into my skis with a click, smear sunburn cream on my face against the hazards of high-altitude sunlight, adjust my goggles, and glide down the broad slope rippled with the bumps or knobs skiers call moguls. I surrender to the moment, totally absorbed by the challenge of the next sharp drop, and by the fantasy of having wings. I am caught in the embrace of adventure. . . .

Another form of gliding and adventure awaited me in the valley almost directly below, where I discovered soaring.

"Flying in general is fun," said Dr. Hans Leitinger, director of the Alpine Gliding School in the town of Zell am See. "But a power plane offers no match to the thrill and beauty of sailing in the sky. In a sailplane, or glider, you have to use skill, intelligence, and even intuition to find the columns or waves of rising air. You must win your power from the wind and air currents."

Hans outlined the range of conditions which make the Alpine region ideal for gliding. He spoke in precise, softly accented English over lunch as we watched Piper Super Cubs tow the long-winged sailplanes aloft to soaring altitude.

I learned that the varied mountain terrain heats the air above it unevenly, creating columns of rising warm air called thermals. The winds sweeping over the mountains produce either a steady updraft along the ridges or the strong airflow of winds surging over mountains in what is known as a wave lift. A fourth kind of lift occurs where the air masses from two valleys meet; the colder current wedges itself under the other, raising the warmer layer to allow sheer line soaring.

At certain seasons the *Föhn* wind blows steadily from the south for days on end, and those are the times for high-altitude flights, up to 30,000 feet. In Innsbruck I had heard many tales of how this warm, dry wind affects people, making them irritable and moody. But the föhn was not the cause of my anxiety: I think planes are marvelous—for other people. As the moment to strap myself into the glider's back seat drew near, I felt like a specter at a feast surrounded by gluttons for punishment.

Hooked to a towplane by a nylon rope, we bumped along the grassy runway. Moments later Hans released the cable and we floated free with only the murmur of wind to mellow the silence. Wheeling effortlessly, we circled up and up in a continuous spiral, riding a thermal for a rise of 1,200 feet. Then we headed across the valley in a gentle downward drift until—*bump whoosh*—we found another thermal. We banked and dipped, playing with the wind, and when Hans turned to ask, "Isn't this beautiful beyond compare?" the odd thing was that I agreed.

Less than ten miles from Zell am See, Austria's east-west Highway One intersects the spectacular Grossglockner road across the Tauern range, largest in Austria. I followed the stream of traffic winding and climbing along this showcase of mountain scenery, and succumbed once again to the spell of snow-clad peaks and granite in the grip of glacial ice—a splendor at once desolate and serene—an image of eternity.

I stopped briefly in Lienz, the small, pretty capital of East Tyrol. For a moment I might have been somewhere along the Mediterranean. The flowerbeds in the plaza sprouted palms, and sidewalk cafes slowed the pace of shoppers and tourists. But I hurried on, for I had an appointment in Kartitsch, a storybook village in the Little Gail Valley, an idyllic drive west along the Drau River.

"A GROUP of us go up the Pfannspitze tonight to see the sun rise over the mountains," said Father Bernhard Hippler as we stopped on a hillside outside Kartitsch to look at the tall wooden racks used to dry hay.

On a working holiday, young Father Hippler had arrived from Innsbruck to substitute for the village priest going on vacation. Since the college students in Kartitsch were his friends at the University of Innsbruck and since his affection for the mountains led him uphill at every opportunity, Father Hippler made the most of the situation by organizing expeditions to the surrounding peaks.

And that is how I found myself slogging up a steep trail at 9 p.m., too weary and out of breath to go on but with no place to stop until we reached the *Hütte* near the top. There was no moon that night, but the sky was carpeted with stars enough to light our rocky path, an ascending wilderness of gray within the black walls of the night. Gottfried Strasser, a theology student on holiday, had set the pace as two by two the seven of us hiked, sang, and yodeled the first hour away.

Warble *"Holla du do lar i o*—that's the place where I put down my things." And you have the ingredients of a yodel. Let your voice ring with laughter and gusto, and then you can really yodel.

A rock thundered down the mountainside. "The loose stones, they are dangerous." Silence.

I labored through the second hour recalling the warning of Ferdl Maier, a mountain guide at the international resort of Kitzbühel since 1929, to people from low altitudes.

"People always down the mountain; then they climb quick up. Then they have trouble." I could still see his suntanned face, etched with the outdoors.

"Comes a man on the Wilder Kaiser two years ago. He goes quick. They found him dead. In the mountains first you have to *klimatisieren.*"

My pounding heart understood.

We finally stopped to rest where the trail broadened into a meadow.

"My uncle died here many years ago," said Luis Ausserlechner, a math and physics student. "He was up here in winter to roll down the bundles of hay stored in the Alpine sheds all over our alms. As usual he held on to the bundle of tumbling hay for a slide down the mountain in the snow. But the hay swept him over a precipice. A plaque just below marks the place where he fell."

"Nur eine Stunde," said Gottfried, helping me up when I showed no sign of stirring.

Another hour. Will they set up a plaque for me, I wondered. Actually a small baroque chapel seemed about right.

I remembered more of Herr Maier's advice. "In climbing always lean away from the hill. Then you can stand on the whole foot, and you don't slip. If you lean to the hill, you are on your toes."

Lean! Lie down, that's what I wanted to do. Even my thoughts came in gasps.

Midnight; and we arrived at the hütte after three long, long hours, but Father Bernhard got us up at four o'clock.

We crossed patches of snow in a wilderness of rock. Here was the rubble left over after Creation. "Luis's brother died climbing that peak over there," said Father Bernhard. So the mountains took their toll even among those who knew and loved them.

A primeval staircase of loose stones led to the summit, at 7,871 feet, enveloped in clouds. I saw no sunrise that day. Instead, I acquired cherished memories of warm-hearted people who delight in friendship and fiercely love their mountain land.

We had a merry breakfast at the hütte—coffee, bacon, *Wurst,* salami, and gallant toasts in a fiery *Schnaps,* "good for the

On Christmas Eve, at Wagrain, Anton Thurner's family gathers in their 300-year-old parlor to open presents. He distributes the gaily-wrapped packages as his wife, Barbara, and a farmhand sort them in the corner. In Austria children believe that Christkindl, the Christ Child himself, not only brings gifts but also decorates the tree for the holiday.

heart." By 8 a.m. the sun had banished the clouds, and we strode down the mountain laughing, gathering pink clusters of *Alprosen* in the bright sunshine and reveling in camaraderie.

Parents, brothers, sisters, aunts, uncles greeted us back in Kartitsch. "But you cannot go until you have eaten," said Gottfried's mother. And I lingered on and on.

With more than a little sadness I left East Tyrol for the lakes of Carinthia. The landscape in this region softens; and the warm, blue-green lakes, the undulating hills, the sunlight filtered through oak forests have a gentle, mild charm.

The Vienna Boys' Choir has chosen the Wörther See for a vacation home. They play and swim until the practice hour at five o'clock. While I waited for them to have their *Jause,* the afternoon snack of coffee and cake or crisp rolls, I rented a sailboat from one of the many marinas. The lap of the water against the hull, the gentle breeze, and lazy look of ripples breaking against the reeded shore—all conspired to make me late, and the boys were already singing when I slipped into the rehearsal hall.

While the languid waters of the Wörther See evoke a calm to dream by, the chill Enns River, foaming and tumbling over boulders and rocks, generates a livelier mood. For Erich Knauss of the Kanu-Club of Schladming a swift current and white water have a special challenge and lure.

"The more rocks, the greater the force of the current, the greater the danger. But for me they are an irresistible temptation," explains Erich, a bookkeeper by profession with a daredevil soul.

"Rivers are graded one to six in difficulty," he told me. "It takes no great skill to paddle down the Danube from the German border to Vienna—an easy run that rates only a one."

I had driven north across Carinthia into densely forested Styria to join him on a stretch of the Enns upstream from the medieval market town of Schladming. This reach of river usually rates a three; in spring, when snowmelt swells the stream, it becomes difficult enough to earn a four.

Even as Erich pushed the rubberized canvas *Faltboot,* a collapsible canoe, into the river, waves slapped at the sides; they splashed water into the narrow, shallow seats before we could fit the canvas covers around us. I sat forward, sealed into place with the slosh of cold water to keep me alert.

Breakers dashed over us as we paddled into the current. But as we bounced and sped away downriver the fever of exhilaration banished the shivers of cold.

Herr Höflinger, president of the canoe club, stood mournfully on the right bank. Three times he had asked me, "Are you sure you can swim?" Indeed I could; but what good would that do, I wondered, in water no more than thigh high and bristling with rocks?

We passed between sloping mountain meadows—vistas of undulating green. Here and there stood lone Styrian farmhouses of weathered wood, and in the distance above a fringe of forest we could see the harsh glare of granite. After half an hour or so we approached a wooden bridge spanning the river, and whom should we see but Herr Höflinger, looking more worried than ever.

All too soon the ten-mile journey ended, but I was looking forward to an engagement with history. I wanted to be in Bad Ischl, a spa in Upper Austria, on August 18 for the *Kaisermesse,* the Imperial Mass commemorating the Emperor's birthday.

The Emperor Franz Josef had died in 1916 after a reign of 68 years, leaving his domains in the midst of the famine and trauma of World War I. But the Habsburg monarch, and the Austro-Hungarian Empire that perished two years after him, lived on in the memories of the silver-haired, aristocratic men and women gathered in the large baroque church at Bad Ischl, where the Emperor had spent his summers.

"It's a nostalgia for the old times," the Baroness Elisabeth Sardagna remarked. "The old Austria was wonderful. Then we were 52 million and now we are 7 million."

Sardagna, an Italian name, echoed the time when the Empire extended from the Adriatic to the forests of southern Poland. The Swarovskis, leading industrialists of Tyrol, came from Bohemia. Gutwinski, Debene, Kövess, Vetsera, Kokoschka are also Austrian names, for the old monarchy was home to Poles, Hungarians, Czechs, Serbs, Slovenes, and Slovaks. It was a realm older than modern nationalism, and it survived for centuries.

After the service, about 400 people lingered outside the church. Courtly and distinguished men bowed and greeted ladies with the formal *"Küss die Hand."* I walked with Captain Louis Krauchenberg, a veteran of the imperial cavalry, frail but elegant at

78, to the Kaiser Villa, the Emperor's hunting lodge nearby. "The Emperor was a passionate hunter," the captain said as we went in. The walls were covered with antlers, each pair — 3,600 in all — mounted on a plaque recording the date and place of the kill.

The house of Habsburg had ruled Austria since 1278, time enough for a dynasty to acquire splendid tastes; but Franz Josef led a simple, even spartan, life amid the elaborate ritual of the court. "The Kaiser ate little, and he ate quickly," the captain told me. "The last ones served at imperial banquets were at a disadvantage, for of course no one could eat after the Kaiser had dined."

Maria Theresia, the Great Empress who reigned from 1740 to 1780, had a vitality, high good humor, and a rich capacity for enjoying life that is more typical of the Austrian character. But perhaps Franz Josef's disciplined, austere ways helped him to endure the many misfortunes that came his way. His brother Maximilian was executed after a three-year reign as Emperor of Mexico; his son Rudolf committed suicide; his wife, the beautiful Empress Elizabeth, wandered restlessly through Europe most of her married life until she died at the hands of an assassin; the Archduke Franz Ferdinand, heir to the throne after Rudolf's death, was shot at Sarajevo — plunging Europe into war.

BUT the Austrian character has been tested many times in the crucible of adversity. Leni Kuborn-Grothe of Kitzbühel, a woman with an elegance and beauty that defy time, typifies its resilience and resourcefulness. "I fled from Vienna after World War II. My husband died, my two children were hungry, and it was very difficult to buy anything. I came to Kitzbühel and designed and sewed belts like these." She showed me her latest creations in velvets, sequins, golden ribbons, rhinestones, and other synthetic gems. "I used fabrics and bits of glitter from heirlooms and my pre-war clothes. I bartered these belts for CARE packages from American soldiers, and sold packages for food."

I recalled that story as I walked from the Kaiser Villa to Zauner's, a pastry shop and coffeehouse that returned me once again to the 19th century. Since 1832 Zauner's has been tempting customers with tarts, tortes, cream rolls, cakes, strudels that defy description. I had to choose from a room-length glass display case — a treasure house of calories — and finally selected apple strudel.

Coffee too is not a simple choice. There is *Mokka,* a strong black brew, usually very sweet; espresso, very strong indeed; the *Einspänner,* black, served in a glass with a blob of whipped cream; *Melange,* a breakfast favorite, half coffee, half milk; *Kapuziner,* coffee with milk and whipped cream. The variety is not surprising, for it is from Austria that coffee conquered most of the West. When the Turks were defeated at Vienna in 1683, they left behind great quantities of coffee beans. A Pole, Johann Kolschitzki, received the beans as a reward for his services in the defense of the city and, in consequence, the first European coffeehouse was born.

Good coffee, good wine, convivial friends, a day in the mountains — these are ingredients of the good life. To these the Austrian adds a profound love of music and beauty. Salzburg, city of baroque churches, of ornate palaces and lavish gardens, of concerts and street theaters, of operas and art exhibits, embodies the soul of Austria.

To this center of the arts, in sight of the mountains, come people from all over the world for the annual Salzburg Festival. Symphony orchestras play morning matinees. Marionettes perform Mozart in the afternoon. Concert music and opera are the sounds of the night. In the fortress castle of Hohensalzburg, perched on a hill overlooking the city, college students and middle-aged technicians, housewives and artisans study painting, sculpture, and architecture. At the 17th-century palace of Hellbrunn, ballet and song make their appearance amid the fountains and grottoes of formal gardens.

And in the Dom Platz, the great square in front of Salzburg's cathedral, Death in a black cape comes to claim Jedermann. Here, a morality play performed outdoors tells the tragedy of Everyman rich in possessions but spiritually bankrupt. As the churchbells toll and the setting sun casts lengthening shadows across the plaza, Jedermann meets adversity without despair.

The poet Ferdinand Sauter, born in Salzburg, wrote an epitaph for himself that perhaps speaks for all Austrians: "Here lies one who had much joy and much sorrow and between them happiness; one rich in experience and poor in worldly goods, who lived without worries and died without trouble." Sauter had mastered the art of living well; and that, I discovered, is a gift the people of the Alps share so graciously with us all. □

Authors and Photographers

National Geographic photographer JAMES P. BLAIR grew up in Mount Lebanon, Pennsylvania, took up skiing in his state's western mountains, studied photography at the Institute of Design in Chicago, recently "learned gravitational pull firsthand on the Cresta Run." He served two years in the Navy and worked as a free lance before joining the Society's staff in 1962; his travels range from Ethiopia to California, Czechoslovakia to Brazil.

Born in Essex, England, WALTER MEAYERS "TOPPY" EDWARDS began his career with the Society in 1933, is now Chief of Pictorial Research for the National Geographic photographic staff. His magazine assignments have included the Alps, France, and Micronesia as well as dozens of American subjects; he now specializes in covering Colorado River country. His photographs illustrate the 1972 Special Publication *Great American Deserts*.

Norwegian by birth, TOR EIGELAND left home at age 16 to go to sea; he studied at McGill University in Montreal, Mexico City College, and the University of Miami in Florida before becoming a free-lance photojournalist — and American citizen. Working out of Beirut, Lebanon, for five years, he now makes his home in Sitges, Spain. His previous assignments for the Society include northern and western areas Down Under for *Australia*, Bedouin tribal life for *Nomads of the World*.

WILLIAM GRAVES, author of the 1970 Special Publication *Hawaii* and a member of the National Geographic Senior Editorial Staff, first explored the Alps as a Foreign Service Officer. A native of Washington, D. C., he earned a B.A. in English from Harvard, served in the Navy during World War II, and reported political events of the Capital before joining the magazine staff in 1956. Recent assignments have taken him to Denmark and to Thailand.

An Army journalist for two years during the Viet Nam era, WILLIAM R. GRAY celebrated his return to civilian life by a six-week winter tour of the entire Alpine region with his wife, Linda. Now weekends often find them climbing, backpacking, and camping in the Appalachians. Born in Washington, D. C., Will received a bachelor's degree in English from Bucknell University; he joined the Special Publications editorial staff as a writer in 1968.

Before coming to the Society in 1958, MARY ANN HARRELL earned a B.A. in English from Wellesley College, an M.A. from the University of North Carolina (her native state), and worked for a farm magazine. She wrote a historical account of the Supreme Court for *Equal Justice Under Law*, produced by the Society as a public service; her Special Publications assignments have included chapters for *Australia* and *Those Inventive Americans*.

ROBERT PAUL JORDAN, member of the National Geographic Senior Editorial Staff and author of *The Civil War*, a 1969 Special Publication, enjoyed the Swiss Alps "as much as any assignment I ever had" — and assignments have taken him all over the world since he came to the Society in 1962. Born in Omaha, Nebraska, he attended Marquette and George Washington Universities, with graduate study at American University, and formerly worked for the *Washington Post*.

ARTHUR P. MILLER, JR., born in Washington, D. C., grew up in New Jersey, graduated from Pennsylvania State University, served as a naval officer in the Pacific during World War II. Earning an M.A. from Columbia University, he made a career in journalism, joining the Society's staff in 1958. For Special Publications he has written of Canada's Maritime Provinces, the Hopi Indians of Arizona, and inventor Charles Goodyear's tragicomic struggles with India rubber.

California born, National Geographic photographer GEORGE F. MOBLEY earned a B.J. degree from the University of Missouri's School of Journalism, served in the Air Force, and worked as a free lance before joining the Society's staff in 1961. A "self-professed nomad at heart," he reported on the Lapps of Norway for Special Publications' *Vanishing Peoples of the Earth* and photographed the Gaduliya Lohars of India for *Nomads of the World*.

A New Yorker by birth, CYNTHIA RUSS RAMSAY earned her B.A. at Hunter College, with graduate study at the University of Pennsylvania. Serving abroad with the U. S. Information Agency, she hiked in the Himalayas; in Iran she taught English in two universities — and explored Middle Eastern mountains. Joining Special Publications in 1966, she was project editor for *Vanishing Peoples of the Earth* and *As We Live and Breathe: The Challenge of Our Environment*.

Index

Illustrations references, including legends, appear in *italics*.

Library of Congress Ⓒ𝕀ℙ data Bibliography: P.
  1. Alps—description and travel—views.
I. National Geographic Society. Washington, D C. Special Publications Division.
DQ823.5.A55   914.94′/′04/   72-75384   ISBN 0-87044-109-4

Acknowledgments

The Special Publications Division is grateful to the persons and organizations named or quoted in this book and to those listed here, for their generous cooperation and assistance: embassy staff, tourist or travel office personnel, and other government officials of the Alpine countries; the Smithsonian Institution; Professor Rado L. Lencek, Columbia University; Veronika Seydel-Rehers, Munich; Professor Rudolf Trümpy, Geologisches Institut, Eidg. Technische Hochschule, Zurich; Professor Franklyn Van Houten, Princeton University.

Additional Reading

The reader may want to consult the *National Geographic Index* for related material, as well as the following recent NATIONAL GEOGRAPHIC articles: Samuel W. Matthews, "This Changing Earth," January 1973; Robert Paul Jordan, "Yugoslavia: Six Republics in One," May 1970. A special supplement map of the Alpine region accompanied the September 1965 issue, with "The Alps: Man's Own Mountains," by Ralph Gray.

  To supplement guidebooks and histories, the following books may be helpful: Nigel Calder, *The Restless Earth;* Marjorie Hope Nicolson, *Mountain Gloom and Mountain Glory;* James Ramsey Ullman, *The Age of Mountaineering.*

Composition for *The Alps* by National Geographic's Phototypographic Division, Carl M. Shrader, Chief; Lawrence F. Ludwig, Assistant Chief. Printed and bound by Fawcett Printing Corp., Rockville, Md. Color separations by Graphic Color Plate, Inc., Stamford, Conn.; The Lanman Company, Alexandria, Va.; and Progressive Color Corp., Rockville, Md.